Big Data
A Tool for Inclusion or Exclusion?

UNDERSTANDING THE ISSUES

FTC REPORT

JANUARY 2016

FEDERAL TRADE COMMISSION

Edith Ramirez, Chairwoman

Julie Brill, Commissioner

Maureen K. Ohlhausen, Commissioner

Terrell McSweeny, Commissioner

Contents

Executive Summary . . . .

I. Introduction 1

II. Life Cycle of Big Data 3

III. Big Data's Benefits and Risks 5

IV. Considerations for Companies in Using Big Data 12
    A. Potentially Applicable Laws 12
        Questions for Legal Compliance 24
    B. Special Policy Considerations Raised by Big Data Research 25
        Summary of Research Considerations. 32

V. Conclusion 33

Appendix:
    Separate Statement of Commissioner Maureen K. Ohlhausen A-1

Executive Summary

We are in the era of big data. With a smartphone now in nearly every pocket, a computer in nearly every household, and an ever-increasing number of Internet-connected devices in the marketplace, the amount of consumer data flowing throughout the economy continues to increase rapidly.

The analysis of this data is often valuable to companies and to consumers, as it can guide the development of new products and services, predict the preferences of individuals, help tailor services and opportunities, and guide individualized marketing. At the same time, advocates, academics, and others have raised concerns about whether certain uses of big data analytics may harm consumers, particularly low-income and underserved populations.

To explore these issues, the Federal Trade Commission ("FTC" or "the Commission") held a public workshop, *Big Data: A Tool for Inclusion or Exclusion?*, on September 15, 2014. The workshop brought together stakeholders to discuss both the potential of big data to create opportunities for consumers and to exclude them from such opportunities. The Commission has synthesized the information from the workshop, a prior FTC seminar on alternative scoring products, and recent research to create this report. Though "big data" encompasses a wide range of analytics, this report addresses only the commercial use of big data consisting of consumer information and focuses on the impact of big data on low-income and underserved populations. Of course, big data also raises a host of other important policy issues, such as notice, choice, and security, among others. Those, however, are not the primary focus of this report.

As "little" data becomes "big" data, it goes through several phases. The life cycle of big data can be divided into four phases: (1) collection; (2) compilation and consolidation; (3) analysis; and (4) use. This report focuses on the fourth phase and discusses the benefits and risks created by the use of big data analytics; the consumer protection and equal opportunity laws that currently apply to big data; research in the field of big data; and lessons that companies should take from the research. Ultimately, this report is intended to educate businesses on important laws and research that are relevant to big data analytics and provide suggestions aimed at maximizing the benefits and minimizing its risks.

Big Data's Benefits and Risks

Big data analytics can provide numerous opportunities for improvements in society. In addition to more effectively matching products and services to consumers, big data can create opportunities for low-income and underserved communities. For example, workshop participants and others have noted that big data is helping target educational, credit, healthcare, and employment opportunities to low-income and underserved populations. At the same time, workshop participants and others have noted how potential inaccuracies and biases might lead to detrimental effects for low-income and underserved populations. For example, participants raised concerns that companies could use big data to exclude low-income and underserved communities from credit and employment opportunities.

Consumer Protection Laws Applicable to Big Data

Workshop participants and commenters discussed how companies can use big data in ways that provide benefits to themselves and society, while minimizing legal and ethical risks. Specifically, they noted that companies should have an understanding of the various laws, including the Fair Credit Reporting Act, equal opportunity laws, and the Federal Trade Commission Act, that may apply to big data practices.

1. Fair Credit Reporting Act

The Fair Credit Reporting Act ("FCRA") applies to companies, known as consumer reporting agencies or CRAs, that compile and sell consumer reports, which contain consumer information that is used or expected to be used for credit, employment, insurance, housing, or other similar decisions about consumers' eligibility for certain benefits and transactions. Among other things, CRAs must implement reasonable procedures to ensure maximum possible accuracy of consumer reports and provide consumers with access to their own information, along with the ability to correct any errors.

Traditionally, CRAs include credit bureaus, employment background screening companies, and other specialty companies that provide particularized services for making consumer eligibility decisions, such as check authorizations or tenant screenings. Some data brokers may also be considered CRAs subject to the FCRA, particularly if they advertise their services for eligibility purposes. The Commission has entered into a number of consent decrees with data brokers that advertise their consumer profiles for employment and tenant screening purposes. Companies that use consumer reports also have obligations under the FCRA.

Workshop panelists and commenters discussed a growing trend in big data, in which companies may be purchasing predictive analytics products for eligibility determinations. Under traditional credit scoring models, companies compare known credit characteristics of a consumer—such as past late payments—with historical data that shows how people with the same credit characteristics performed over time in meeting their credit obligations. Similarly, predictive analytics products may compare a known characteristic of a consumer to other consumers with the same characteristic to predict whether that consumer will meet his or her credit obligations. The difference is that, rather than comparing a traditional credit characteristic, such as debt payment history, these products may use non-traditional characteristics—such as a consumer's zip code, social media usage, or shopping history—to create a report about the creditworthiness of consumers that share those non-traditional characteristics, which a company can then use to make decisions about whether that consumer is a good credit risk. The standards applied to determine the applicability of the FCRA in a Commission enforcement action, however, are the same.

Only a fact-specific analysis will ultimately determine whether a practice is subject to or violates the FCRA, and as such, companies should be mindful of the law when using big data analytics to make FCRA-covered eligibility determinations.

2. Equal Opportunity Laws

Companies should also consider a number of federal equal opportunity laws, including the Equal Credit Opportunity Act ("ECOA"), Title VII of the Civil Rights Act of 1964, the Americans with Disabilities Act, the Age Discrimination in Employment Act, the Fair Housing Act, and the Genetic Information Nondiscrimination Act. These laws prohibit discrimination based on protected characteristics such as race, color, sex or gender, religion, age, disability status, national origin, marital status, and genetic information.

Of these laws, the FTC enforces ECOA, which prohibits credit discrimination on the basis of race, color, religion, national origin, sex, marital status, age, or because a person receives public assistance. To prove a violation of ECOA, plaintiffs typically must show "disparate treatment" or "disparate impact." Disparate treatment occurs when a creditor treats an applicant differently based on a protected characteristic. For example, a lender cannot refuse to lend to single persons or offer less favorable terms to them than married persons even if big data analytics show that single persons are less likely to repay loans than married persons. Disparate impact occurs when a company employs facially neutral policies or practices that have a disproportionate adverse effect or impact on a protected class, unless those practices or policies further a legitimate business need that cannot reasonably be achieved by means that are less disparate in their impact. For example, if a company makes credit decisions based on consumers' zip codes, such decisions may have a disparate impact on particular ethnic groups because certain ethnic groups are concentrated in particular zip codes. Accordingly, the practice may be a violation of ECOA. The analysis turns on whether the decisions have a disparate impact on a protected class and are not justified by a legitimate business necessity. Even if evidence shows the decisions are justified by a business necessity, if there is a less discriminatory alternative, the decisions may still violate ECOA.

Workshop discussions focused on whether advertising could implicate equal opportunity laws. In most cases, a company's advertisement to a particular community for a credit offer that is open to all to apply is unlikely, by itself, to violate ECOA, absent disparate treatment or an unjustified disparate impact in subsequent lending. Nevertheless, companies should proceed with caution in this area. For advertisements relating to credit products, companies should look to Regulation B, which is the implementing regulation for ECOA. It prohibits creditors from making oral or written statements, in advertising or otherwise, to applicants or prospective applicants that would discourage on a prohibited basis a reasonable person from making or pursuing an application. With respect to prescreened solicitations, Regulation B also requires creditors to maintain records of the solicitations and the criteria used to select potential recipients. Advertising and marketing practices could impact a creditor's subsequent lending patterns and the terms and conditions of the credit received by borrowers, even if credit offers are open to all who apply. In some cases, the Department of Justice has cited a creditor's advertising choices as evidence of discrimination.

Ultimately, as with the FCRA, whether a practice is unlawful under equal opportunity laws is a case-specific inquiry, and as such, companies should proceed with caution when their practices could result in disparate treatment or have a demonstrable disparate impact based on protected characteristics.

3. The Federal Trade Commission Act

Workshop participants and commenters also discussed the applicability of Section 5 of the Federal Trade Commission Act ("FTC Act"), which prohibits unfair or deceptive acts or practices, to big data analytics. Companies engaging in big data analytics should consider whether they are violating any material promises to consumers—whether that promise is to refrain from sharing data with third parties, to provide consumers with choices about sharing, or to safeguard consumers' personal information—or whether they have failed to disclose material information to consumers. In addition, companies that maintain big data on consumers should take care to reasonably secure consumers' data. Further, at a minimum, companies must not sell their big data analytics products to customers if they know or have reason to know that those customers will use the products for fraudulent or discriminatory purposes. The inquiry will be fact-specific, and in every case, the test will be whether the company is offering or using big data analytics in a deceptive or unfair way.

Research on Big Data

Workshop participants, academics, and others also addressed the ways big data analytics could affect low-income, underserved populations, and protected groups. Some pointed to research that demonstrates that there is a potential for incorporating errors and biases at every stage—from choosing the data set used to make predictions, to defining the problem to be addressed through big data, to making decisions based on the results of big data analysis—which could lead to potential discriminatory harms. Others noted that these concerns are overstated or simply not new, and emphasized that rather than disadvantaging minorities, big data can create opportunities for low-income and underserved populations.

To maximize the benefits and limit the harms of big data, the Commission encourages companies to consider the following questions raised by research in this area:

- **How representative is your data set?** Companies should consider whether their data sets are missing information about certain populations, and take steps to address issues of underrepresentation and overrepresentation. For example, if a company targets services to consumers who communicate through an application or social media, they may be neglecting populations that are not as tech-savvy.

- **Does your data model account for biases?** Companies should consider whether biases are being incorporated at both the collection and analytics stages of big data's life cycle, and develop strategies to overcome them. For example, if a company has a big data algorithm that only considers applicants from "top tier" colleges to help them make hiring decisions, they may be incorporating previous biases in college admission decisions.

- **How accurate are your predictions based on big data?** Companies should remember that while big data is very good at detecting correlations, it does not explain which correlations are meaningful. A prime example that demonstrates the limitations of big data analytics is Google Flu Trends, a machine-learning algorithm for predicting the number of flu cases based on Google search terms. While, at first, the algorithms appeared to create accurate predictions of where the flu was more prevalent, it generated highly inaccurate estimates over time. This could be because the algorithm failed to take into account certain variables. For example, the algorithm may not have taken into account that people would be more likely to search for flu-related terms if the local news ran a story on a flu outbreak, even if the outbreak occurred halfway around the world.

- **Does your reliance on big data raise ethical or fairness concerns?** Companies should assess the factors that go into an analytics model and balance the predictive value of the model with fairness considerations. For example, one company determined that employees who live closer to their jobs stay at these jobs longer than those who live farther away. However, another company decided to exclude this factor from its hiring algorithm because of concerns about racial discrimination, particularly since different neighborhoods can have different racial compositions.

The Commission encourages companies to apply big data analytics in ways that provide benefits and opportunities to consumers, while avoiding pitfalls that may violate consumer protection or equal opportunity laws, or detract from core values of inclusion and fairness. For its part, the Commission will continue to monitor areas where big data practices could violate existing laws, including the FTC Act, the FCRA, and ECOA, and will bring enforcement actions where appropriate. The Commission will also continue to examine and raise awareness about big data practices that could have a detrimental impact on low-income and underserved populations, and promote the use of big data that has a positive impact on such populations.

Federal Trade Commission

I. Introduction

The era of big data has arrived. While companies historically have collected and used information about their customer interactions to help improve their operations, the expanding use of online technologies has greatly increased the amount of consumer data that flows throughout the economy. In many cases, when consumers engage digitally—whether by shopping, visiting websites, paying bills, connecting with family and friends through social media, using mobile applications, or using connected devices, such as fitness trackers or smart televisions—companies collect information about their choices, experiences, and individual characteristics. The analysis of this consumer information is often valuable to companies and to consumers, as it provides insights into market-wide tastes and emerging trends, which can guide the development of new products and services. It is also valuable to predict the preferences of specific individuals, help tailor services, and guide individualized marketing of products and services.

The term "big data" refers to a confluence of factors, including the nearly ubiquitous collection of consumer data from a variety of sources, the plummeting cost of data storage, and powerful new capabilities to analyze data to draw connections and make inferences and predictions.[1]

A common framework for characterizing big data relies on the "three Vs," the volume, velocity, and variety of data, each of which is growing at a rapid rate as technological advances permit the analysis and use of this data in ways that were not possible previously.[2] Volume refers to the vast quantity of data that can be gathered and analyzed effectively. The costs of collecting and storing data continue to drop dramatically. And the ability to access millions of data points increases the predictive power of consumer data analysis.

---

1 *See, e.g.*, Exec. Office of the President, Big Data: Seizing Opportunities, Preserving Values 2–3 (2014) [hereinafter "White House May 2014 Report"], http://www.whitehouse.gov/sites/default/files/docs/big_data_privacy_report_5.1.14_final_print.pdf; Jim Thatcher, *Living on Fumes: Digital Footprints, Data Fumes, and the Limitations of Spatial Big Data*, 8 Int'l J. Of Commc'n 1765, 1767–69 (2014), http://ijoc.org/index.php/ijoc/article/view/2174/1158. *See also* Comment #00018 from Persis Yu, Nat'l Consumer L. Ctr., to Fed. Trade Comm'n, attached report at 10 (Aug. 15, 2014), https://www.ftc.gov/system/files/documents/public_comments/2014/08/00018-92374.pdf.

2 *See, e.g.*, Transcript of Big Data: A Tool for Inclusion or Exclusion?, in Washington, D.C. (Sept. 15, 2014), at 15 (Solon Barocas), 32 (Joseph Turow), 40–41 (Joseph Turow), 261 (Christopher Wolf) [hereinafter Big Data Tr.], https://www.ftc.gov/system/files/documents/public_events/313371/bigdata-transcript-9_15_14.pdf. *See also* White House May 2014 Report, *supra* note 1, at 4–5; Comment #00067 from Mark MacCarthy, Software & Info. Indus. Assoc., to Fed. Trade Comm'n 2 (Oct. 31, 2014), https://www.ftc.gov/system/files/documents/public_comments/2014/10/00067-92918.pdf; Comment #00065 from Jules Polonetsky & Christopher Wolf, Future of Privacy Forum, to Fed. Trade Comm'n 2 (Oct. 31, 2014), https://www.ftc.gov/system/files/documents/public_comments/2014/10/00065-92921.pdf; Comment #00049 from Martin Abrams, Info. Accountability Found., to Fed. Trade Comm'n 3–4 & n.6, https://www.ftc.gov/system/files/documents/public_comments/2014/10/00049-92780.pdf; Comment #00031 from M. Gary LaFever & Ted Myerson, anonos, to Fed. Trade Comm'n 1 (Aug. 21, 2014), https://www.ftc.gov/system/files/documents/public_comments/2014/08/00031-92442.pdf. Others suggest that there is a "fourth V," veracity, to denote the accuracy and integrity of data used. *See, e.g.*, Brian Gentile, *The New Factors of Production and the Rise of Data-Driven Applications*, Forbes (Oct. 31, 2011), http://www.forbes.com/sites/ciocentral/2011/10/31/the-new-factors-of-production-and-the-rise-of-data-driven-applications/.

Velocity is the speed with which companies can accumulate, analyze, and use new data. Technological improvements allow companies to harness the predictive power of data more quickly than ever before, sometimes instantaneously.[3]

Variety means the breadth of data that companies can analyze effectively. Companies can now combine very different, once unlinked, kinds of data—either on their own or through data brokers or analytics firms—to infer consumer preferences and predict consumer behavior, for example.

Together, the three Vs allow for more robust research and correlation. Previously, finding a representative data sample sufficient to produce statistically significant results could be very difficult and expensive. Today, the present scope and scale of data collection enables cost-effective, substantial research of even obscure or mundane topics (e.g., the amount of foot traffic in a park at different times of day).

Big data can produce tremendous benefits for society, such as advances in medicine, education, health, and transportation, and in many instances, without using consumers' personally identifiable information. Big data also can allow companies to improve their offerings, provide consumers with personalized goods and services, and match consumers with products they are likely to be interested in. At the same time, advocates, academics, and others have raised concerns about whether certain uses of big data analytics may harm consumers. For example, if big data analytics incorrectly predicts that particular consumers are not likely to respond to prime credit offers, certain types of educational opportunities, or job openings requiring a college degree, companies may miss a chance to reach individuals that desire this information. In addition, if big data analytics incorrectly predicts that particular consumers are not good candidates for prime credit offers, educational opportunities, or certain lucrative jobs, such educational opportunities, employment, and credit may never be offered to these consumers. Some fear that such incorrect predictions could perpetuate existing disparities.

To examine these issues, the Federal Trade Commission ("FTC" or "the Commission") held a public workshop, *Big Data: A Tool for Inclusion or Exclusion?*, on September 15, 2014.[4] In particular, the workshop explored the potential impact of big data on low-income and underserved populations. The workshop brought together academics, government representatives, consumer advocates, industry representatives, legal practitioners, and others to discuss the potential of big data to create opportunities for consumers or exclude them from such opportunities. The workshop consisted of four panels addressing the following topics: (1) current uses of big data; (2) potential uses of big data; (3) the application of equal opportunity and consumer protection laws to big data; and (4) best practices to enhance consumer protection in the use of big data. The Commission also received sixty-five public comments on these issues from private citizens, industry representatives, trade groups, consumer and privacy advocates, think tanks, and academics.

---

3   WHITE HOUSE MAY 2014 REPORT, *supra* note 1, at 5.

4   The materials from the workshop are available on the FTC website at http://www.ftc.gov/news-events/events-calendar/2014/09/big-data-tool-inclusion-or-exclusion.

The Commission has synthesized the discussions and comments from the workshop—along with the record from a prior FTC seminar on alternative scoring products[5] and recent research—to create this report, which focuses on the impact of big data on low-income and underserved populations. The report is divided into four sections. First, the report describes the "life cycle" of big data and how "little" data turns into big data. Second, it discusses some of the benefits and risks created by the use of big data. Third, it describes some of the consumer protection laws that currently apply to big data. Finally, it discusses certain research in the field of big data and lessons that companies should take from the research in order to help them maximize the benefits of big data while mitigating risks. Importantly, though the term "big data" encompasses a wide range of analytics, this report addresses only the commercial use of big data consisting of consumer information.[6]

II. Life Cycle of Big Data

The life cycle of big data can be divided into four phases: (1) collection; (2) compilation and consolidation; (3) data mining and analytics; and (4) use.[7]

As to the first step, not all data starts as big data. Rather, companies collect bits of data from a variety of sources.[8] For example, as consumers browse the web or shop online, companies can track and link their activities. Sometimes consumers log into services or identify themselves when they make a purchase. Other

---

5   On March 19, 2014, the Commission hosted a seminar on alternative scoring products and received nine public comments in connection with the seminar. *Spring Privacy Series: Alternative Scoring Products*, FED. TRADE COMM'N (Mar. 19, 2014), http://www.ftc.gov/news-events/events-calendar/2014/03/spring-privacy-series-alternative-scoring-products.

6   The report does include some examples from non-commercial fields, but it is intended to guide companies as they use big data about consumers.

7   *See, e.g.*, Nat'l Consumer L. Ctr. Comment #00018, *supra* note 1, attached report at 11–12. In May 2014, the Commission released a report studying data brokers, which focused on the first three phases of the life cycle of big data. FED. TRADE COMM'N, DATA BROKERS: A CALL FOR TRANSPARENCY AND ACCOUNTABILITY (2014) [hereinafter "DATA BROKERS REPORT"], https://www.ftc.gov/system/files/documents/reports/data-brokers-call-transparency-accountability-report-federal-trade-commission-may-2014/140527databrokerreport.pdf.

8   *See generally* Comment #00055 from Daniel Castro, Ctr. for Data Innovation, to Fed. Trade Comm'n (Oct. 23, 2014), https://www.ftc.gov/system/files/documents/public_comments/2014/10/00055-92856.pdf; Comment #00026 from Daniel Castro, Ctr. for Data Innovation, to Fed. Trade Comm'n (Aug. 15, 2014), https://www.ftc.gov/system/files/documents/public_comments/2014/08/00026-92395.pdf; Comment #00024 from Alvaro Bedoya, Ctr. on Privacy & Tech. at Geo. L., to Fed. Trade Comm'n (Aug. 15, 2014), https://www.ftc.gov/system/files/documents/public_comments/2014/08/00024-92434.pdf; Nat'l Consumer L. Ctr. Comment #00018, *supra* note 1; Comment #00016 from James Steyer, Common Sense Media, to Fed. Trade Comm'n (Aug. 15, 2014), https://www.ftc.gov/system/files/documents/public_comments/2014/08/00016-92371.pdf; Comment #00015 from Nathan Newman, N.Y.U. Info. L. Inst., to Fed. Trade Comm'n (Aug. 15, 2014), https://www.ftc.gov/system/files/documents/public_comments/2014/08/00015-92370.pdf; Comment #00010 from Thomas Lenard, Tech. Pol'y Inst., to Fed. Trade Comm'n (July 28, 2014), https://www.ftc.gov/system/files/documents/public_comments/2014/07/00010-92280.pdf; Comment #00003 from Jeff Chester, Ctr. for Dig. Democracy, & Edmund Mierzwinski, U.S. PIRG Educ. Fund, to Fed. Trade Comm'n (May 9, 2014), https://www.ftc.gov/system/files/documents/public_comments/2014/05/00003-90097.pdf.

times, techniques such as tracking cookies,[9] browser or device fingerprinting,[10] and even history sniffing[11] identify who consumers are, what they do, and where they go. In the mobile environment, companies track and link consumers' activities across applications as another method of gathering information about their habits and preferences. More broadly, cross-device tracking offers the ability to interact with the same consumer across her desktop, laptop, tablet, wearable, and smartphone, using both online and offline information.[12] Companies also are gathering data about consumers across the Internet of Things—the millions of Internet-connected devices that are in the market.[13] Finally, data collection occurs offline as well, for example, through loyalty programs, warranty cards, surveys, sweepstakes entries, and even credit card purchases.[14]

After collection, the next step in the life cycle of big data is compilation and consolidation. Commercial entities that compile data include online ad networks, social media companies, and large banks or retailers.[15] One important category of commercial entities that compile and consolidate data is data brokers. They combine data from disparate sources to build profiles about individual consumers. Indeed, some data brokers store billions of data elements on nearly every U.S. consumer.[16]

The third step is data analytics. One form of analytics is descriptive—the objective is to uncover and summarize patterns or features that exist in data sets.[17] By contrast, predictive data analytics refers to the use

---

[9] Tracking cookies are a specific type of cookie that is distributed, shared, and read across two or more unrelated websites for the purpose of gathering information or presenting customized data to a consumer. *See Tracking Cookie*, SYMANTEC, https://www.symantec.com/security_response/writeup.jsp?docid=2006-080217-3524-99 (last visited Dec. 29, 2015).

[10] "'Browser fingerprinting' is a method of tracking web browsers by the configuration and settings information they make visible to websites, rather than traditional tracking methods" such as cookies. *Panopticlick: Is Your Browser Safe Against Tracking?*, ELEC. FRONTIER FOUND., https://panopticlick.eff.org/about#browser-fingerprinting (last visited Dec. 29, 2015).

[11] History sniffing is the practice of tracking which sites a user has or has not visited. *See* Ben Schott, *History Sniffing*, N.Y. TIMES (Dec. 8, 2010), http://schott.blogs.nytimes.com/2010/12/08/history-sniffing/?_r=0. *See also* Brian Krebs, *What You Should Know About History Sniffing*, KREBS ON SEC. (Dec. 6, 2010), http://krebsonsecurity.com/2010/12/what-you-should-know-about-history-sniffing/.

[12] In November 2015, the Commission held a workshop to study the various alternative techniques used to track consumers across their devices. *See Cross-Device Tracking*, FED. TRADE COMM'N (Nov. 16, 2015), https://www.ftc.gov/news-events/events-calendar/2015/11/cross-device-tracking.

[13] In January 2015, the Commission released a staff report entitled, INTERNET OF THINGS: PRIVACY & SECURITY IN A CONNECTED WORLD, recommending steps businesses can take to enhance and protect consumers' privacy and security as it relates to Internet-connected devices. FED. TRADE COMM'N, INTERNET OF THINGS: PRIVACY AND SECURITY IN A CONNECTED WORLD (2015), https://www.ftc.gov/system/files/documents/reports/federal-trade-commission-staff-report-november-2013-workshop-entitled-internet-things-privacy/150127iotrpt.pdf.

[14] *See, e.g.*, DATA BROKERS REPORT, *supra* note 7, at 11–15.

[15] *See generally* Nat'l Consumer L. Ctr. Comment #00018, *supra* note 1; N.Y.U. Info. L. Inst. Comment #00015, *supra* note 8; Ctr. for Dig. Democracy & U.S. PIRG Educ. Fund Comment #00003, *supra* note 8.

[16] *See, e.g.*, DATA BROKERS REPORT, *supra* note 7, at 46–47.

[17] *See, e.g.*, Big Data Tr. 17 (Solon Barocas) ("[W]e can define data mining as the automated process of extracting useful patterns from large data sets, and in particular, patterns that can serve as a basis for subsequent decision making."). *See also* JURE LESKOVEC ET AL., MINING OF MASSIVE DATA SETS 1, 1 (2014), http://www.mmds.org/ (characterizing "data mining" as "the construction of a *statistical model*, that is, an underlying distribution from which the visible data is drawn") (emphasis in original).

of statistical models to generate new data.[18] Developing and testing the models that find patterns and make predictions can require the collection and use of copious amounts of data.[19] In a market context, a common purpose of big data analytics is to draw inferences about consumers' likely choices. Companies may decide to adopt big data analytics to better understand consumers, potentially by using data to attribute to an individual the qualities of those who appear statistically similar, e.g., those who have made similar decisions in similar situations in the past. Thus, a retail firm might use data on its customers' past purchases, web searches, shopping habits, and prices paid to create a statistical model of consumers' purchases at different prices. With that model, the retailer could then compare a prospective consumer's characteristics or past purchases, web searches, and location information to predict how likely the consumer is to purchase a product at various price points.

The final step in the life cycle of big data is use. The Commission's May 2014 report entitled *Data Brokers: A Call for Transparency and Accountability* focused on the first three steps in the life cycle of big data within that industry—collection, compilation, and analytics.[20] It discussed how information gathered for one purpose (e.g., paying for goods and services) could be compiled and analyzed for other purposes, such as for marketing or risk mitigation. In contrast, this report focuses on certain *uses* of big data. It examines the question of how companies use big data to help consumers and the steps they can take to avoid inadvertently harming consumers through big data analytics.

III. Big Data's Benefits and Risks

Companies have been analyzing data from their own customer interactions on a smaller scale for many years, but the era of big data is still in its infancy.[21] As a result, mining large data sets to find useful, non-obvious patterns is a relatively new but growing practice in marketing, fraud prevention, human resources, and a variety of other fields. Companies are still learning how to deal with big data and unlock its potential while avoiding unintended or unforeseen consequences.[22]

Appropriately employing big data algorithms on data of sufficient quality can provide numerous opportunities for improvements in society. In addition to the market-wide benefits of more efficiently matching products and services to consumers, big data can create opportunities for low-income and

---

18 *See, e.g.*, Galit Shmueli, *To Explain or Predict?*, 25 STATISTICAL SCI. 289, 291 (2010), http://www.stat.berkeley.edu/~aldous/157/Papers/shmueli.pdf. *See also* Mike Wu, *Big Data Reduction 2: Understanding Predictive Analytics*, SCI. OF SOCIAL BLOG (Mar. 26, 2013 9:41 AM), http://community.lithium.com/t5/Science-of-Social-blog/Big-Data-Reduction-2-Understanding-Predictive-Analytics/ba-p/79616 ("[P]redictive analytics is all about using *data you have* to predict *data that you don't have*.") (emphases in original).

19 *Cf.* Comment #00014 from Pam Dixon & Robert Gellman, World Privacy Forum, to Fed. Trade Comm'n 8 (Aug. 14, 2014), https://www.ftc.gov/policy/public-comments/2014/08/14/comment-00014.

20 *See generally* DATA BROKERS REPORT, *supra* note 7.

21 *See, e.g.*, Big Data Tr. 31–32 (Gene Gsell), 32–33 (Joseph Turow), 34 (Mallory Duncan), 107–08 (Pamela Dixon).

22 *See, e.g.*, Big Data Tr. 31–32 (Gene Gsell), 32–33 (Joseph Turow), 78 (danah boyd), 233 (Michael Spadea).

underserved communities.[23] Workshop participants and others have noted that big data is already being used to:

- **Increase educational attainment for individual students.** Educational institutions have used big data techniques to identify students for advanced classes who would otherwise not have been eligible for such classes based on teacher recommendations alone.[24] These institutions have also used big data techniques to help identify students who are at risk of dropping out and in need of early intervention strategies.[25] Similarly, organizations have used big data analytics to demonstrate how certain disciplinary practices, such as school suspensions, affect African-American students far more than Caucasian students, thereby partly explaining the large discrepancy between the graduation rates of these two groups.[26]

- **Provide access to credit using non-traditional methods.** Companies have used big data to provide alternative ways to score populations that were previously deemed unscorable.[27] For example, LexisNexis has created an alternative credit score called RiskView.[28] This product relies on traditional public record information, such as foreclosures and bankruptcies, but it also includes educational history, professional licensure data, and personal property ownership data. Thus, consumers who may not have access to traditional credit, but, for instance, have a professional license, pay rent on time, or own a car, may be given better access to credit than they otherwise would have.[29]

---

23 *See, e.g.*, Big Data Tr. 83–85 (Mark MacCarthy), 250–51 (Christopher Wolf). *See generally* Comment #00076 from William Kovacs, U.S. Chamber of Commerce, to Fed. Trade Comm'n (Oct. 31, 2014), https://www.ftc.gov/system/files/documents/public_comments/2014/10/00076-92936.pdf; Comment #00073 from Michael Beckerman, The Internet Assoc., to Fed. Trade Comm'n (Oct. 31, 2014), https://www.ftc.gov/system/files/documents/public_comments/2014/10/00073-92923.pdf; Comment #00066 from Carl Szabo, NetChoice, to Fed. Trade Comm'n (Oct. 31, 2014), https://www.ftc.gov/system/files/documents/public_comments/2014/10/00066-92920.pdf; Comment #00063 from Peggy Hudson, Direct Mktg. Assoc., to Fed. Trade Comm'n (Oct. 31, 2014), https://www.ftc.gov/system/files/documents/public_comments/2014/10/00063-92909.pdf; Ctr. for Data Innovation Comment #00055, *supra* note 8; Comment #00027 from Jules Polonetsky, Future of Privacy Forum, to Fed. Trade Comm'n (Aug. 15, 2014), https://www.ftc.gov/system/files/documents/public_comments/2014/08/00027-92420.pdf; Ctr. for Data Innovation Comment #00026, *supra* note 8; Comment #00017 from Mike Zaneis, Interactive Advert. Bureau, to Fed. Trade Comm'n (Aug. 15, 2014), https://www.ftc.gov/system/files/documents/public_comments/2014/08/00017-92372.pdf; Tech. Pol'y Inst. Comment #00010, *supra* note 8.

24 *See, e.g.*, Big Data Tr. 47–48 (Gene Gsell). *Cf.* Ctr. for Data Innovation Comment #00055, *supra* note 8, attached report entitled, The Rise of Data Poverty in America, at 4–6.

25 *See, e.g.*, Big Data Tr. 84–85 (Mark MacCarthy). *See also* Software & Info. Indus. Assoc. Comment #00067, *supra* note 2, at 6–7; Ctr. for Data Innovation Comment #00026, *supra* note 8, at 2.

26 *See, e.g.*, Big Data Tr. 250 (Christopher Wolf). *See also* Future of Privacy Forum Comment #00027, *supra* note 23, attached report entitled, Big Data: A Tool for Fighting Discrimination and Empowering Groups, at 9.

27 *See, e.g.*, Big Data Tr. 49–51 (Gene Gsell), 83–84 (Mark MacCarthy), 102–06 (Stuart Pratt), 231–32 (Michael Spadea). *See also* Software & Info. Indus. Assoc. Comment #00067, *supra* note 2, at 5–6; Tech. Pol'y Inst. Comment #00010, *supra* note 8, at 5–6 & attached report entitled, Big Data, Privacy and the Familiar Solutions, at 7.

28 *See, e.g.*, Software & Info. Indus. Assoc. Comment #00067, *supra* note 2, at 5–6.

29 *See, e.g.*, *Rent Reporting for Credit Building Consulting*, Credit Builders All., http://creditbuildersalliance.org/rent-reporting-credit-building-consulting (last visited Dec. 22, 2015).

Furthermore, big data algorithms could help reveal underlying disparities in traditional credit markets and help companies serve creditworthy consumers from any background.[30]

- **Provide healthcare tailored to individual patients' characteristics.** Organizations have used big data to predict life expectancy, genetic predisposition to disease, likelihood of hospital readmission, and likelihood of adherence to a treatment plan in order to tailor medical treatment to an individual's characteristics.[31] This, in turn, has helped healthcare providers avoid one-size-fits-all treatments and lower overall healthcare costs by reducing readmissions.[32] Ultimately, data sets with richer and more complete data should allow medical practitioners more effectively to perform "precision medicine," an approach for disease treatment and prevention that considers individual variability in genes, environment, and lifestyle.[33]

- **Provide specialized healthcare to underserved communities.** IBM, for example, has worked with hospitals to develop an Oncology Diagnosis and Treatment Advisor. This system synthesizes vast amounts of data from textbooks, guidelines, journal articles, and clinical trials to help physicians make diagnoses and identify treatment options for cancer patients. In rural and low-income areas, where there is a shortage of specialty providers, IBM's Oncology Diagnosis and Treatment Advisor can provide underserved communities with better access to cancer care and lower costs.[34]

- **Increase equal access to employment.** Companies have used big data to help promote a more diverse workforce.[35] Google, for example, recognized that its traditional hiring process was resulting in a homogenous work force. Through analytics, Google identified issues with its hiring process, which included an emphasis on academic grade point averages and "brainteaser" questions

---

30 *See, e.g.*, Ctr. for Data Innovation Comment #00055, *supra* note 8, attached report entitled, THE RISE OF DATA POVERTY IN AMERICA, at 9. *See generally* Fair Isaac Corp., *Can Alternative Data Expand Credit Access*, INSIGHTS WHITE PAPER No. 90 (2015), http://www.fico.com/en/latest-thinking/white-papers/can-alternative-data-expand-credit-access (finding that alternative scoring can help lenders safely and responsibly extend credit to many of the more than fifty million U.S. adults who do not currently have FICO scores).

31 *See, e.g.*, Ctr. for Data Innovation Comment #00026, *supra* note 8, at 2. *See also* Shannon Pettypiece & Jordan Robertson, *Hospitals are Mining Patients' Credit Card Data to Predict Who Will Get Sick*, BLOOMBERG (July 3, 2014), http://www.bloomberg.com/bw/articles/2014-07-03/hospitals-are-mining-patients-credit-card-data-to-predict-who-will-get-sick.

32 *See, e.g.*, Ctr. for Data Innovation Comment #00055, *supra* note 8, attached report entitled, THE RISE OF DATA POVERTY IN AMERICA, at 6–8; Future of Privacy Forum Comment #00027, *supra* note 23, attached report entitled, BIG DATA: A TOOL FOR FIGHTING DISCRIMINATION AND EMPOWERING GROUPS, at 4; Ctr. for Data Innovation Comment #00026, *supra* note 8, at 2. *Cf.* Software & Info. Indus. Assoc. Comment #00067, *supra* note 2, at 4–5.

33 *See, e.g.*, David Shaywitz, *New Diabetes Study Shows How Big Data Might Drive Precision Medicine*, FORBES (Oct. 30, 2015), http://www.forbes.com/sites/davidshaywitz/2015/10/30/new-diabetes-study-shows-how-big-data-might-drive-precision-medicine/.

34 *See, e.g.*, Big Data Tr. 84 (Mark MacCarthy). *See also* Software & Info. Indus. Assoc. Comment #00067, *supra* note 2, at 4.

35 *See, e.g.*, Big Data Tr. 126 (Mark MacCarthy), 251 (Christopher Wolf); Software & Info. Indus. Assoc. Comment #00067, *supra* note 2, at 7; Future of Privacy Forum Comment #00027, *supra* note 23, attached report entitled, BIG DATA: A TOOL FOR FIGHTING DISCRIMINATION AND EMPOWERING GROUPS, at 1–2. *See also* Lauren Weber, *Can This Algorithm Find Hires of a Certain Race?*, WALL ST. J. (Apr. 30, 2014), http://blogs.wsj.com/atwork/2014/04/30/can-this-algorithm-find-hires-of-a-certain-race/.

during interviews. Google then modified its interview practices and began asking more structured behavioral questions (e.g., how would you handle the following situation?).[36] This new approach helped ensure that potential interviewer biases had less effect on hiring decisions.

While recognizing these potential benefits, some researchers and others have expressed concern that the use of big data analytics to make predictions may exclude certain populations from the benefits society and markets have to offer. This concern takes several forms. First, some workshop participants and commenters expressed concerns about the quality of data, including its accuracy, completeness, and representativeness.[37] Another concern is that there are uncorrected biases in the underlying consumer data.[38] For example, one academic has argued that hidden biases in the collection, analysis, and interpretation stages present considerable risks.[39] If the process that generated the underlying data reflects biases in favor of or against certain types of individuals, then some statistical relationships revealed by that data could perpetuate those biases. When not recognized and addressed, poor data quality can lead to inaccurate predictions, which in turn can lead to companies erroneously denying consumers offers or benefits. Although the use of inaccurate or biased data and analysis to justify decisions that have harmed certain populations is not new,[40] some commenters worry that big data analytics may lead to wider propagation of the problem and make it more difficult for the company using such data to identify the source of discriminatory effects and address it.[41]

---

36   *See, e.g.*, Big Data Tr. 251 (Christopher Wolf). *See also* Future of Privacy Forum Comment #00027, *supra* note 23, attached report entitled, BIG DATA: A TOOL FOR FIGHTING DISCRIMINATION AND EMPOWERING GROUPS, at 2; David Amerland, *3 Ways Big Data Changed Google's Hiring Process*, FORBES (Jan. 21, 2014), http://www.forbes.com/sites/netapp/2014/01/21/big-data-google-hiring-process/; Adam Bryant, *In Head-Hunting, Big Data May Not Be Such a Big Deal*, N.Y. TIMES (June 19, 2013), http://www.nytimes.com/2013/06/20/business/in-head-hunting-big-data-may-not-be-such-a-big-deal.html?pagewanted=1&%2359&adxnnlx=1371813584-7rFFVvpSQsf/NlnpuVABGQ&%2359;_r=3.

37   *See, e.g.*, Big Data Tr. 21–22 (Solon Barocas), 29–31 (David Robinson), 100–02 (Dr. Nicol Turner-Lee); Transcript of Spring Privacy Series: Alternative Scoring Products, in Washington, D.C. (Mar. 19, 2014), at 44–45 (Pamela Dixon) [hereinafter Alternative Scoring Tr.], https://www.ftc.gov/system/files/documents/public_events/182261/alternative-scoring-products_final-transcript.pdf. *See also* Ctr. for Data Innovation Comment #00055, *supra* note 8, attached report entitled, THE RISE OF DATA POVERTY IN AMERICA, at 2; Nat'l Consumer L. Ctr. Comment #00018, *supra* note 1, attached report entitled, BIG DATA: A BIG DISAPPOINTMENT FOR SCORING CONSUMER RISK, at 9, 27; Ctr. for Dig. Democracy & U.S. PIRG Educ. Fund Comment #00003, *supra* note 8, at 2. *See generally* Nir Grinberg et al., *Extracting Diurnal Patterns of Real World Activity from Social Media* (The 9th Int'l Conference on Web and Social Media, Working Paper 2013), http://sm.rutgers.edu/pubs/Grinberg-SMPatterns-ICWSM2013.pdf.

38   *See, e.g.*, Big Data Tr. 23–25 (Solon Barocas); Alternative Scoring Tr. 93 (Claudia Perlich). *See also* Cynthia Dwork & Deirdre Mulligan, *It's Not Privacy and It's Not Fair*, 66 STAN. L. REV. ONLINE 35, 36–37 (2013), http://www.stanfordlawreview.org/sites/default/files/online/topics/DworkMullliganSLR.pdf.

39   Kate Crawford, *The Hidden Biases in Big Data*, HARV. BUS. REV. (2013), https://hbr.org/2013/04/the-hidden-biases-in-big-data.

40   *See generally* Helen F. Ladd, *Evidence on Discrimination in Mortgage Lending*, 12(2) J. OF ECON. PERSPECTIVES 41 (1998), https://www.aeaweb.org/atypon.php?return_to=/doi/pdfplus/10.1257/jep.12.2.41.

41   *See, e.g.*, Big Data Tr. 40–41 (Joseph Turow).

Second, while big data may be highly effective in showing correlations, it is axiomatic that correlation is not causation.[42] Indeed, with large enough data sets, one can generally find some meaningless correlations. For example, in eighteen out of the past twenty U.S. Presidential elections, if the Washington, D.C. professional football team won its last home game before the election, the incumbent's party continued to hold the presidency; if the team lost that last home game, the out-of-office party unseated the incumbent party.[43] Other examples of spurious correlations abound.[44] If companies use correlations to make decisions about people without understanding the underlying reasons for the correlations, those decisions might be faulty and could lead to unintended consequences or harm for consumers and companies.

Ultimately, all of these concerns feed into the larger concern about whether big data may be used to categorize consumers in ways that can result in exclusion of certain populations. Workshop participants and others have noted how potential inaccuracies and biases might lead to detrimental effects for low-income and underserved populations.[45] According to these commenters, particular uses of big data may:

- **Result in more individuals mistakenly being denied opportunities based on the actions of others.** Participants raised concerns that big data can lead to decision-making based on the actions of others with whom consumers share some characteristics.[46] Several commenters explained that some credit card companies have lowered a customer's credit limit, not based on the customer's payment history, but rather based on analysis of other customers with a poor repayment history that had shopped at the same establishments where the customer had shopped.[47] Indeed, one credit card company settled FTC allegations that it failed to disclose its practice of rating consumers as having a greater credit risk because they used their cards to pay for marriage counseling, therapy, or tire-repair services, based on its experiences with other consumers and their repayment histories.[48] Using this type of a statistical model might reduce the cost of credit for some individuals, but may also result

---

42 *See generally* John Aldrich, *Correlations Genuine and Spurious in Pearson and Yule*, 10(4) STATISTICAL SCI. 364 (1995), http://www.jstor.org/stable/2246135. *See also Correlation*, XKCD, https://xkcd.com/552/ (last visited Dec. 29, 2015).

43 *Winning Tradition*, SNOPES.COM, http://www.snopes.com/politics/ballot/redskins.asp (last visited Dec. 29, 2015).

44 *See, e.g.*, *Spurious Correlations*, TYLERVIGEN.COM, http://www.tylervigen.com/spurious-correlations (last visited Dec. 29, 2015) (showing a variety of spurious correlations, including, for example, a historical correlation between the annual number of people who have drowned by falling into a swimming pool and the annual number of films in which Nicolas Cage has appeared).

45 *See, e.g.*, Big Data Tr. 222 (Jeremy Gillula). *See generally* Nat'l Consumer L. Ctr. Comment #00018, *supra* note 1; Common Sense Media Comment #00016, *supra* note 8; N.Y.U. Info. L. Inst. Comment #00015, *supra* note 8; Ctr. for Dig. Democracy & U.S. PIRG Educ. Fund Comment #00003, *supra* note 8.

46 *See, e.g.*, Big Data Tr. 42–44 (danah boyd). *See also* Comment #00078 from Seeta Peña Gangadharan et al., New Am.'s Open Tech. Inst., to Fed. Trade Comm'n, attached report entitled, THE NETWORKED NATURE OF ALGORITHMIC DISCRIMINATION, at 53–57 (Oct. 31, 2014), https://www.ftc.gov/system/files/documents/public_comments/2014/10/00078-92938.pdf.

47 *See, e.g.*, Nat'l Consumer L. Ctr. Comment #00018, *supra* note 1, at 27–28; N.Y.U. Info. L. Inst. Comment #00015, *supra* note 8, at 6.

48 *See* FTC v. CompuCredit Corp., No. 1:08-cv-1976-BBM-RGV (N.D. Ga. June 10, 2008), https://www.ftc.gov/sites/default/files/documents/cases/2008/12/081219compucreditstiporder.pdf. *See also* Danielle Keats Citron & Frank A. Pasquale III, *The Scored Society: Due Process for Automated Predictions*, 89 WASH. L. REV. 1, 4 (2014), http://ssrn.com/abstract=2376209.

in some creditworthy consumers being denied or charged more for credit than they might otherwise have been charged.[49]

- **Create or reinforce existing disparities.** Participants raised concerns that when big data is used to target ads, particularly for financial products, low-income consumers who may otherwise be eligible for better offers may never receive them.[50]

- **Expose sensitive information.** Participants also raised concerns about the potential exposure of characteristics that people may view as sensitive.[51] For example, one study combined data on Facebook "Likes" and limited survey information to determine that researchers could accurately predict a male user's sexual orientation 88 percent of the time; a user's ethnic origin 95 percent of time; and whether a user was Christian or Muslim (82 percent), a Democrat or Republican (85 percent), or used alcohol, drugs, or cigarettes (between 65 percent and 75 percent).[52]

- **Assist in the targeting of vulnerable consumers for fraud.** Unscrupulous companies can use big data to offer misleading offers or scams to the most vulnerable prospects.[53] According to public reports, unscrupulous companies can obtain lists of people who reply to sweepstakes offers and thus are more likely to respond to enticements, as well as lists of "suffering seniors" who are identified as having Alzheimer's or similar maladies.[54] Big data analytics allows companies to more easily and accurately identify such vulnerable prospects.

- **Create new justifications for exclusion.** Big data analytics may give companies new ways to attempt to justify their exclusion of certain populations from particular opportunities. For example, one big data analytics study showed that "people who fill out online job applications using browsers that did not come with the computer . . . but had to be deliberately installed (like Firefox or Google's

---

49 *See, e.g.*, Alternative Scoring Tr. 96 (Edmund Mierzwinski).

50 *See, e.g.*, Big Data Tr. 228–30 (Christopher Calabrese); Alternative Scoring Tr. 64–67 (Ashkan Soltani). *See also* Ctr. for Dig. Democracy & U.S. PIRG Educ. Fund Comment #00003, *supra* note 8, at 10–11, 18–29.

51 *See, e.g.*, Big Data Tr. 89–90 (Pamela Dixon), 71–72 (Kristin Amerling); Alternative Scoring Tr. 76 (Pamela Dixon), 92 (Ashkan Soltani). *See also* Am.'s Open Tech. Inst. Comment #00078, *supra* note 46, attached report entitled, HEALTH PRIVACY ONLINE: PATIENTS AT RISK, at 11–16; Ctr. on Privacy & Tech. at Geo. L. Comment #00024, *supra* note 8, at 9; DATA BROKERS REPORT, *supra* note 7, at 19–21, 47.

52 *See* Michal Kosinski et al., *Private Traits and Attributes Are Predictable From Digital Records of Human Behavior*, 110 PROCEEDINGS OF THE NAT'L ACAD. OF SCIS. 5802, 5803–04 (2013), http://www.pnas.org/content/110/15/5802.abstract. *See also* Jon Green, *Facebook Knows You're Gay Before You Do*, AM. BLOG (Mar. 20, 2013), http://americablog.com/2013/03/facebook-might-know-youre-gay-before-you-do.html.

53 *See, e.g.*, Comment #00080 from David Robinson, Robinson + Yu, to Fed. Trade Comm'n 8–9 (Oct. 31, 2014), https://www.ftc.gov/system/files/documents/public_comments/2014/10/00080-92939.pdf; N.Y.U. Info. L. Inst. Comment #00015, *supra* note 8, at 6–7. *See also* FTC v. LeapLab, LLC, No. 2:14-cv-02750 (D. Ariz. filed Dec. 22, 2014), https://www.ftc.gov/system/files/documents/cases/141223leaplabcmpt.pdf.

54 *See, e.g.*, N.Y.U. Info. L. Inst. Comment #00015, *supra* note 8, at 6–7.

Chrome) perform better and change jobs less often."⁵⁵ If an employer were to use this correlation to refrain from hiring people who used a particular browser, they could be excluding qualified applicants for reasons unrelated to the job at issue.

- **Result in higher-priced goods and services for lower income communities.** Some commentators have raised concerns about potential effects on prices on lower income communities.⁵⁶ For example, research has shown that online companies may charge consumers in different zip codes different prices for standard office products.⁵⁷ If such pricing results in consumers in poorer neighborhoods having to pay more for online products than consumers in affluent communities, where there is more competition from brick-and-mortar stores, these poorer communities would not realize the full competition benefit of online shopping.⁵⁸

- **Weaken the effectiveness of consumer choice.** Some researchers have argued that, even when companies offer consumers choices about data collection, the companies may still use big data to draw inferences about consumers who choose to restrict the collection of their data.⁵⁹ Indeed, using data from consumers who opt in or decline to opt out, big data algorithms can still be employed to infer information about similarly-situated individuals who chose not to share their data.⁶⁰

---

55 *See, e.g.*, Mark Andrejevic, *The Big Data Divide*, 8 Int'l J. of Commc'n 1673, 1681 (2014), http://ijoc.org/index.php/ijoc/article/download/2161/1163. *See also Robot Recruiters*, Economist (Apr. 6, 2013), http://www.economist.com/news/business/21575820-how-software-helps-firms-hire-workers-more-efficiently-robot-recruiters.

56 *See, e.g.*, Lauren Kirchner, *When Big Data Becomes Bad Data*, ProPublica (Sept. 2, 2015), https://www.propublica.org/article/when-big-data-becomes-bad-data (finding that areas with high density of Asian residents are often charged more for the Princeton Review's online SAT tutoring). *But see* Exec. Office of the President, Big Data and Differential Pricing 17 (2015), [hereinafter White House Feb. 2015 Report], http://www.whitehouse.gov/sites/default/files/whitehouse_files/docs/Big_Data_Report_Nonembargo_v2.pdf ("[I]f historically disadvantaged groups are more price-sensitive than the average consumer, profit-maximizing differential pricing should work to their benefit" in competitive markets.). This holds true for relatively competitive markets. However, the report also points out that disadvantaged groups may face less competitive markets and be penalized by differential pricing. *Id.* Economists have shown that price discrimination can improve or reduce consumer welfare, depending on how price discrimination is implemented. *See generally* Dirk Bergemann et al., *The Limits of Price Discrimination*, 105(3), Am. Econ. Rev. 921 (2015), https://www.aeaweb.org/articles.php?doi=10.1257/aer.20130848. Economists have also shown that greater price discrimination could raise or reduce the intensity of competition. *See generally* Kenneth S. Corts, *Third-Degree Price Discrimination in Oligopoly: All-Out Competition and Strategic Commitment*, RAND J. of Econs. 306 (1998), http://www.jstor.org/stable/2555890?seq=1#page_scan_tab_contents.

57 *See, e.g.*, Alternative Scoring Tr. 62–64 (Askhan Soltani). *See also* Jennifer Valentino-Devries et al., *Websites Vary Prices, Deals Based on Users' Information*, Wall St. J. (Dec. 24, 2012), http://www.wsj.com/articles/SB10001424127887323777204578189391813881534.

58 *See, e.g.*, Nat'l Consumer L. Ctr Comment #00018, *supra* note 1, at 27; N.Y.U. Info. L. Inst. Comment #00015, *supra* note 8, at 4–5. *See also* Alternative Scoring Tr. 62–64 (Ashkan Soltani). For an example of differential pricing using IP addresses, see Valentino-Devries et al., *supra* note 57. For an example of steering based on the type of operating system, see Martha C. White, *Orbitz Shows Higher Prices to Mac Users*, Time (June 26, 2012), http://business.time.com/2012/06/26/orbitz-shows-higher-prices-to-mac-users/.

59 Solon Barocas & Helen Nissenbaum, *Big Data's End Run Around Anonymity and Consent*, in Privacy, Big Data, and the Public Good: Frameworks for Engagement 44, 61–63 (Julia Lane et al. eds., 2014).

60 *Id.*

As these examples show, big data offers companies the opportunity to facilitate inclusion or exclusion. Companies can use big data to advance education, credit, and employment opportunities for low-income communities or to exclude them from these opportunities. They can use big data to target products to those who are most interested or to target products in ways that could exclude certain populations. The remainder of this report is intended to guide companies on some of the laws that may apply when using big data, raise awareness about the ethical implications of using big data, and to highlight potential biases that companies should consider as they use big data.

IV. Considerations for Companies in Using Big Data

The challenge for companies is not *whether* they should use big data; indeed, the reality of today's marketplace is that big data now fuels the creation of innovative products and systems that consumers and companies quickly are coming to rely upon and expect. Rather, the challenge is *how* companies can use big data in a way that benefits them and society, while minimizing legal and ethical risks.

In assessing risks, companies should first have an understanding of the laws that may apply to big data practices. Second, they should be aware of important research in the field of big data aimed at identifying potential biases and inaccuracies. This section provides a starting point for companies using big data analytics. It is not intended to provide an exhaustive list of considerations. Rather, companies using big data should consider the issues raised in this report as they engage in big data practices and build on the questions posed to examine the legal, privacy, and ethical implications of their work.

A. Potentially Applicable Laws

The following section describes some of the laws that may apply to big data practices.[61] Although the laws discussed do not address every potential misuse, as noted above, this report is not intended to identify

---

61 *See, e.g.*, Big Data Tr. 38 (Kristin Amerling), 45–47, 69–70 (David Robinson), 95, 120–22 (Stuart Pratt), 99, 108 (Pamela Dixon), 268 (Christopher Calabrese), 163–213 (Leonard Chanin, Carol Miaskoff, Montserrat Miller, C. Lee Peeler, and Peter Swire in conversation); Alternative Scoring Tr. 36–37, 71 (Stuart Pratt). *See generally* Comment #00075 from Michelle De Mooy, Ctr. for Democracy & Tech., to Fed. Trade Comm'n (Oct. 31, 2014), https://www.ftc.gov/system/files/documents/public_comments/2014/10/00075-92928.pdf; Comment #00068 from Julie Kearney & Alexander Reynolds, Consumer Elecs. Assoc., to Fed. Trade Comm'n (Oct. 31, 2014), https://www.ftc.gov/system/files/documents/public_comments/2014/10/00068-92917.pdf; Software & Info. Indus. Assoc. Comment #00067, *supra* note 2; Future of Privacy Forum Comment #00065, *supra* note 2; Direct Mktg. Assoc. Comment #00063, *supra* note 23; Comment #00062 from David Hoffman, Intel Corp., to Fed. Trade Comm'n (Oct. 31, 2014), https://www.ftc.gov/system/files/documents/public_comments/2014/10/00062-92887.pdf; Comment #00061 from Jeff Chester, Ctr. for Dig. Democracy, & Edmund Mierzwinski, U.S. PIRG Educ. Fund, to Fed. Trade Comm'n (Oct. 29, 2014), https://www.ftc.gov/system/files/documents/public_comments/2014/10/00061-92886.pdf; Comment #00059 from Laura Murphy & Rachel Goodman, Am. Civil Liberties Union, to Fed. Trade Comm'n (Oct. 27, 2014), https://www.ftc.gov/system/files/documents/public_comments/2014/10/00059-92874.pdf; Ctr. for Data Innovation Comment #00026, *supra* note 8; Comment #00025 from Dennis Hirsch, Cap. Univ. L. Sch., to Fed. Trade Comm'n (Aug. 15, 2014), https://www.ftc.gov/system/files/documents/public_comments/2014/08/00025-92435.pdf; Comment #00021 from U.S. Chamber of Commerce, to Fed. Trade Comm'n (Aug. 15, 2014), https://www.ftc.gov/system/files/documents/public_comments/2014/08/00021-92389.pdf; Comment #00020 from Jim Halpert, Internet Commerce Coal., to Fed. Trade Comm'n (Aug. 15, 2014), https://

legal or policy gaps; rather, it attempts to guide companies on laws, such as the Fair Credit Reporting Act, equal opportunity laws, and the Federal Trade Commission Act, that may apply to big data practices.[62]

1. The Fair Credit Reporting Act

The FTC has the authority to enforce compliance with the Fair Credit Reporting Act ("FCRA").[63] The FCRA applies to companies, known as consumer reporting agencies or CRAs, that compile and sell consumer reports, which contain consumer information that is used or expected to be used for credit, employment, insurance, housing, or other similar decisions about consumers' eligibility for certain benefits and transactions.[64] Among other things, CRAs must implement reasonable procedures to ensure maximum possible accuracy of consumer reports[65] and provide consumers with access to their own information, along with the ability to correct any errors.[66] CRAs can only provide consumer reports to those entities that will use them for certain specified permissible purposes, such as for credit, employment, insurance, or housing eligibility determinations.[67]

Traditionally, CRAs include credit bureaus, employment background screening companies, and other specialty companies that provide particularized services for making consumer eligibility decisions, such as check authorizations or tenant screenings. Some data brokers that compile non-traditional information, including social media information, may also be considered CRAs subject to the FCRA, as demonstrated by the Commission's enforcement actions. For example, the Commission entered into a consent decree with online data broker Spokeo to resolve allegations that the company violated the FCRA.[68] As set forth in the FTC's complaint, Spokeo assembled personal information from hundreds of online and offline data sources, including social networks, and merged that data to create detailed personal profiles, including name, address, age range, hobbies, ethnicity, and religion, and marketed these profiles for use by human resources

---

www.ftc.gov/system/files/documents/public_comments/2014/08/00020-92376.pdf; Comment #00019 from Michael Beckerman, Internet Ass'n, to Fed. Trade Comm'n (Aug. 15, 2014), https://www.ftc.gov/system/files/documents/public_comments/2014/08/00019-92375.pdf; Nat'l Consumer L. Ctr. Comment #00018, *supra* note 1; Interactive Advert. Bureau Comment #00017, *supra* note 23; World Privacy Forum Comment #00014, *supra* note 19; Ctr. for Dig. Democracy & U.S. PIRG Educ. Fund Comment #00003, *supra* note 8.

62 This discussion articulates considerations relevant to the Commission's exercise of its enforcement authority. Though this section discusses certain federal laws, companies should also be aware that other federal laws, as well as state and local laws, may apply to their big data practices. They should review these laws in jurisdictions where they operate.

63 15 U.S.C. §§ 1681–1681x (2014).

64 *Id.* § 1681a(f) & (d). As discussed further below, the FCRA also applies to users of consumer reports and those who furnish consumer reports to CRAs.

65 *Id.* § 1681e(b).

66 *Id.* § 1681g–1681j.

67 *Id.* §1681b(a).

68 United States v. Spokeo, Inc., No. 2-12-cv-05001-MMM-SH (C.D. Cal. June 12, 2012), https://www.ftc.gov/sites/default/files/documents/cases/2012/06/120612spokeoorder.pdf. *See also* Press Release, Fed. Trade Comm'n, Spokeo to Pay $800,000 to Settle FTC Charges Company Allegedly Marketed Information to Employers and Recruiters in Violation of FCRA (June 12, 2012), http://www.ftc.gov/news-events/press-releases/2012/06/spokeo-pay-800000-settle-ftccharges-company-allegedly-marketed.

departments in making hiring decisions.[69] Based on the allegations that the company marketed consumer profiles specifically for employment purposes, the Commission charged that Spokeo was subject to, but had failed to comply with, the FCRA. Accordingly, the FTC entered into a consent decree that required Spokeo to pay $800,000 in civil penalties.

In another matter, the Commission alleged that the data broker Instant Checkmate advertised potential uses of its consumer data for employment and tenant screening purposes, both through its website and through blog posts, but did not comply with the FCRA.[70] According to the complaint, the company used a Google AdWords campaign to display ads for its services that would appear in search results when consumers sought background checks on "nannies," "babysitters," "maids," and "housekeepers." Thus, the Commission alleged that the company was subject to the FCRA, entered into a consent order to ensure future compliance, and obtained $550,000 in civil penalties.[71] In both *Spokeo* and *Instant Checkmate*, the companies included a disclaimer on their websites stating that they were not CRAs and that users could not use their data for eligibility purposes. These disclaimers were not effective in insulating the companies from FTC enforcement. As these cases demonstrate, the scope of the FCRA extends beyond traditional credit bureaus.

Companies that use consumer reports also have obligations under the FCRA. They must, among other things, provide consumers with "adverse action" notices if the companies use the consumer report information to deny credit, insurance, employment, housing, or certain other covered benefits.[72] Similarly, companies that use consumer reports must provide "risk-based pricing" notices if they charge consumers more to obtain credit or insurance based on consumer report information.[73] The purpose of both types of notices is to enable consumers to check their consumer reports and correct any inaccuracies.[74] The Commission has brought actions against various companies for violation of these provisions.[75] For example,

---

[69] Complaint at 3–4, *Spokeo*, No. 2-12-cv-05001-MMM-SH (C.D. Cal. filed June 7, 2012), https://www.ftc.gov/sites/default/files/documents/cases/2012/06/120612spokeocmpt.pdf.

[70] Complaint, United States v. Instant Checkmate, Inc., No. 3:14-cv-00675-H-JMA (S.D. Cal. filed Mar. 24, 2014), https://www.ftc.gov/system/files/documents/cases/140409instantcheckmatecmpt.pdf. *See also* Press Release, Fed. Trade Comm'n, Two Data Brokers Settle FTC Charges That They Sold Consumer Data without Complying with Protections Required under the Fair Credit Reporting Act (Apr. 9, 2014), https://www.ftc.gov/news-events/press-releases/2014/04/two-data-brokers-settle-ftc-charges-they-sold-consumer-data.

[71] *Instant Checkmate*, No. 3:14-cv-00675-H-JMA (S.D. Cal. Apr. 1, 2014), https://www.ftc.gov/system/files/documents/cases/140409instantcheckmateorder.pdf.

[72] *See* 15 U.S.C. § 1681m(a). When using consumer reports for employment purposes, companies must also provide consumers with "pre-adverse action notices" before taking any adverse action. *See id.* § 1681b(b)(3).

[73] *See id.* § 1681m(h); 12 C.F.R. §§ 1022.70–1022.75 (2015); FTC Duties of Creditors Regarding Risk-Based Pricing Rule, 16 C.F.R. § 640 (2015).

[74] *See Using Consumer Reports for Credit Decisions: What to Know About Adverse Action and Risk-Based Pricing Notices*, FED. TRADE COMM'N (Dec. 2013), https://www.ftc.gov/tips-advice/business-center/guidance/using-consumer-reports-credit-decisions-what-know-about-adverse.

[75] *See, e.g.*, Complaint, United States. v. Rail Terminal Servs., LLC, No. 09-cv-1111(MJP) (W.D. Wash. filed Aug.11, 2009), https://www.ftc.gov/sites/default/files/documents/cases/2013/08/090806rtscmpt.pdf; Complaint, United States. v. Quality

in 2013, the FTC brought an action against Time Warner Cable because it used a consumer report to determine whether to require deposits on consumers' cable bills.[76] The complaint alleged that consumers who were charged a deposit should have received a risk-based pricing notice informing them that the charge was based on information in their consumer report. The consent order barred Time Warner Cable from future violations of the Risk-Based Pricing Rule and required the company to pay $1.9 million in civil penalties.[77] In addition, in 2015, the Commission brought an action against Sprint alleging that the company failed to give proper risk-based pricing notices to consumers who were placed in a program for customers with lower credit scores and charged an extra monthly fee.[78] The consent order requires Sprint to pay a $2.95 million penalty and to give timely notice to consumers placed in such a program.[79]

The FCRA, however, does not apply to companies when they use data derived from their own relationship with their customers for purposes of making decisions about them.[80] But if an unaffiliated firm regularly evaluates companies' own data and provides the evaluations to the companies for eligibility determinations, the unaffiliated firm would likely be acting as a CRA, each company would likely be a user of consumer reports, and all of these entities would be subject to Commission enforcement under the FCRA.

Workshop panelists and commenters discussed a growing trend in big data, in which companies may be purchasing predictive analytics products for eligibility determinations.[81] Under traditional credit scoring

---

Terminal Servs., LLC, No. 09-cv-01853-CMA-BNB (D. Colo. filed Aug. 11, 2009), https://www.ftc.gov/sites/default/files/documents/cases/2009/08/090806ptscmpt.pdf.

76 Complaint, United States v. Time Warner Cable, Inc., No. 13-cv-8998 (S.D.N.Y. filed Dec. 19, 2013), https://www.ftc.gov/sites/default/files/documents/cases/131219timewarnercmpt.pdf. *See also* Press Release, Fed. Trade Comm'n, Time Warner Cable to Pay $1.9 Million Penalty for Violating Risk-Based Pricing Rule (Dec. 19, 2013), https://www.ftc.gov/news-events/press-releases/2013/12/time-warner-cable-pay-19-million-penalty-violating-risk-based.

77 *Time Warner Cable*, No. 13-cv-8998 (S.D.N.Y. Dec. 20, 2013), https://www.ftc.gov/sites/default/files/documents/cases/131219timewarnerstip.pdf.

78 Complaint at 7–8, United States v. Sprint Corp., No. 2:15-cv-9340 (D. Kan. filed Oct. 21, 2015), https://www.ftc.gov/system/files/documents/cases/151021sprintcmpt.pdf. *See also* Press Release, Fed. Trade Comm'n, Sprint Will Pay $2.95 Million Penalty to Settle FTC Charges It Violated Fair Credit Reporting Act (Oct. 21, 2015), https://www.ftc.gov/news-events/press-releases/2015/10/sprint-will-pay-295-million-penalty-settle-ftc-charges-it.

79 The settlement also requires Sprint to send corrected risk-based pricing notices to consumers who received incomplete notices from the company. *See Sprint*, No. 2:15-cv-9340 (D. Kan. Oct. 21, 2015), https://www.ftc.gov/system/files/documents/cases/151021sprintstip.pdf.

80 15 U.S.C. § 1681a(d)(2)(A)(i). *See also* FED. TRADE COMM'N, 40 YEARS OF EXPERIENCE WITH THE FAIR CREDIT REPORTING ACT: AN FTC STAFF REPORT WITH SUMMARY OF INTERPRETATIONS 1, 23–24 (2011) [hereinafter 40 YEARS FCRA REPORT], https://www.ftc.gov/sites/default/files/documents/reports/40-years-experience-fair-credit-reporting-act-ftc-staff-report-summary-interpretations/110720fcrareport.pdf ("Reports limited to transactions or experiences between the consumer and the entity making the report are not consumer reports. An opinion that is based only on transactions or experiences between the consumer and the reporting entity is also within the exception.").

81 *See, e.g.*, Big Data Tr. 38 (Kristin Amerling), 69–70 (David Robinson), 99–100 (Pamela Dixon); Alternative Scoring Tr. 100–101 (Pamela Dixon). *See also* Nat'l Consumer L. Ctr. Comment #00018, *supra* note 1, at 20–23; World Privacy Forum Comment #00014, *supra* note 19, at 19–21; Ctr. for Dig. Democracy & U.S. PIRG Educ. Fund Comment #00003, *supra* note 8, at 13–15; Comment #00006 from Jeff Chester, Ctr. for Dig. Democracy, & Edmund Mierzwinski,

models, companies compare known credit characteristics of a consumer—such as past late payments—with historical data that shows how people with the same credit characteristics performed over time in meeting their credit obligations. Similarly, predictive analytics products may compare a known characteristic of a consumer to other consumers with the same characteristic to predict whether that consumer will meet his or her credit obligations. The difference is that, rather than comparing a traditional credit characteristic, such as debt payment history, these products may use non-traditional characteristics—such as a consumer's zip code, social media usage, or shopping history—to create a report about the creditworthiness of consumers that share those non-traditional characteristics, which a company can then use to make decisions about whether that consumer is a good credit risk.[82] The standards applied to determine the applicability of the FCRA, however, are the same.

In exercising its enforcement authority, the Commission looks to the FCRA's definition of a "consumer report." The FCRA defines a consumer report as a communication from a CRA (1) bearing on a consumer's personal characteristics or mode of living[83] (2) that "is used or expected to be used . . . for the purpose of serving as a factor in establishing *the* consumer's eligibility."[84] Under this definition, the communication must be prepared or provided to others to make an eligibility determination about a particular consumer.

Suppose a company asks a consumer to provide her zip code and information about her social media and shopping behavior on a credit application, strips the consumer's identifying information, and sends the application to an analytics firm. The firm then analyzes the creditworthiness of people in the same zip code with similar social media and shopping behaviors as the consumer and provides that analysis—be it, for example, in the form of a score, a grade, or a recommendation—to the company, knowing that it is to be used for a credit decision. Because the company is using information about the consumer to generate an analysis of a group that shares some characteristics with the consumer and then is using that analysis to make a decision about the consumer, the Commission would likely regard the analysis to be a consumer report, and FCRA requirements and protections would likely apply.[85]

U.S. PIRG Educ. Fund, to Fed. Trade Comm'n (Mar. 18, 2014), https://www.ftc.gov/system/files/documents/public_comments/2014/03/00006-89085.pdf.

82 *See, e.g.*, Big Data Tr. 69–70 (David Robinson) (noting that these "thinly aggregated scores . . . may be used to lower [consumers'] credit limits"); 99–100 (Pamela Dixon) (noting that these scores are "problematic for ensuring privacy and fairness" because they rely on "[un]regulated data"); Alternative Scoring Tr. 94 (Pamela Dixon) (describing "cohort scoring," which is a type of score based on a consumer's social media friends). *See also* World Privacy Forum Comment #00014, *supra* note 19, at 32–38. *But see supra* text accompanying notes 27–30 (explaining how big data analytics can be used to expand credit availability).

83 As noted in *Trans Union Corp. v. FTC*, this part of the test is not a very demanding one, for almost any information about consumers arguably bears on their personal characteristics or mode of living. 81 F.3d 228, 231 (D.C. Cir. 1996).

84 15 U.S.C. § 1681a(d)(1) (emphasis added).

85 In 2011, FTC staff issued the 40 Years FCRA Report. In that report, staff stated that "[i]nformation that does not identify a specific consumer does not constitute a consumer report even if the communication is used in part to determine eligibility." 40 Years FCRA Report, *supra* note 80, at 20. The Commission does not believe that this statement is accurate. If a report is crafted for eligibility purposes with reference to a particular consumer or set of particular consumers (e.g., those that have

In contrast, if a company uses an analytics firm's report simply to inform its general policies, then the Commission would likely not regard the report to be a consumer report under the FCRA because such a general report does not relate to a particular consumer. For example, if an analytics firm's report simply provides an "aggregate credit score" for every zip code in the United States, a company finds the report through a search engine, and the company uses the report to inform its policies, the Commission would likely not consider the analytics firm's report to be a consumer report or the analytics firm to be a CRA.[86]

As noted above, it is well settled under the FCRA that when a company denies a consumer credit, or charges a higher price for credit, based on information from a CRA, the company must provide the consumer with an adverse action notice. But a creditor may still have obligations under the FCRA even in cases where the creditor obtains information from a company other than a CRA. Section 615(b) of the FCRA provides that, when a company denies a consumer credit, or charges a higher price for credit, based on information from a person *other than a CRA*, the consumer may request, in writing, that the company disclose to him or her the nature of the information leading to the denial or increase in charge.[87] Thus, continuing with the example above, even if a store finds a general analytics company report through a search engine and then uses the report to inform its credit granting policies, the store would have to disclose the nature of the report upon the consumer's request if the consumer's application for credit is denied or the charge for such credit is increased as a result of reliance on the report.

Only a fact-specific analysis will ultimately determine whether a practice is subject to or violates the FCRA, and as such, companies should be mindful of the law when using big data analytics to make FCRA-covered eligibility determinations.

2. Equal Opportunity Laws

When engaging in big data analytics, companies should also consider federal equal opportunity laws, including the Equal Credit Opportunity Act ("ECOA"),[88] Title VII of the Civil Rights Act of 1964,[89]

---

applied for credit), the Commission will consider the report a consumer report even if the identifying information of the consumer has been stripped.

86 Companies that determine eligibility based on zip codes should exercise caution. Such a practice could still implicate equal opportunity laws, if that policy has a disproportionate adverse effect or impact on a protected class, unless those practices or policies further a legitimate business need that cannot reasonably be achieved by means that are less disproportionate in their impact. See discussion *infra* Part IV.A.2.

87 *See* 15 U.S.C. § 1681m(b).

88 15 U.S.C. §§ 1691 *et seq.* (2014). In addition to prohibiting discrimination, ECOA and Regulation B include other requirements that may be implicated by business practices that utilize big data analytics. Informing credit applicants about adverse actions related to applications for credit and identifying the specific reasons an adverse action was taken may be challenging when those reasons implicate big data analytics. *See* 12 C.F.R. § 1002.9. Lenders may also need to review Regulation B requirements on how information is obtained and retained in the credit application process. *See* 12 C.F.R. § 1002.5(b)–(d), 1002.12(a)(2).

89 42 U.S.C. §§ 2000e *et seq.* (2014). The Civil Rights Act of 1964 also applies to education, voting, and public accommodations.

the Americans with Disabilities Act,[90] the Age Discrimination in Employment Act ("ADEA"),[91] the Fair Housing Act ("FHA"),[92] and the Genetic Information Nondiscrimination Act ("GINA").[93] These laws prohibit discrimination based on protected characteristics such as race, color, sex or gender, religion, age, disability status, national origin, marital status, and genetic information.[94]

Companies should review these laws and take steps to ensure their use of big data analytics complies with the discrimination prohibitions that may apply. This section discusses some examples of relevant considerations under these laws related to employment and credit, as highlighted in the workshop.

To prove a violation of federal equal credit or employment opportunity laws, plaintiffs typically must show "disparate treatment" or "disparate impact."[95] Disparate treatment occurs when an entity, such as a creditor or employer, treats an applicant differently based on a protected characteristic such as race or national origin.[96] Systemic disparate treatment occurs when an entity engages in a pattern or practice of differential treatment on a prohibited basis.[97] In some cases, the unlawful differential treatment could be based on big data analytics.[98] For example, an employer may not disfavor a particular protected group because big data analytics show that members of this protected group are more likely to quit their jobs within a five-year period.[99] Similarly, a lender cannot refuse to lend to single persons or offer less favorable terms to them than married persons even if big data analytics show that single persons are less likely to repay loans than married persons. Evidence of such violations could include direct evidence of the reasons for the company's choices, or circumstantial evidence, such as significant statistical disparities in outcomes for protected groups that are unexplained by neutral factors.

---

90 42 U.S.C. §§ 12101 *et seq.* (2014).

91 29 U.S.C. §§ 621 *et seq.* (2014).

92 42 U.S.C. §§ 3601 *et seq.* (2014).

93 42 U.S.C. §§ 2000ff *et seq.* (2014). GINA also applies to health insurance.

94 A number of different agencies have the authority to enforce the various equal opportunity laws. The Equal Employment Opportunity Commission, for example, is responsible for enforcing Title VII of the Civil Rights Act of 1964 (along with the Department of Justice ("DOJ")), the Age Discrimination in Employment Act of 1967, and GINA. The Department of Housing and Urban Development and the DOJ enforce the FHA. The FTC, DOJ, and the Consumer Financial Protection Bureau ("CFPB"), among other agencies, enforce ECOA and its implementing Regulation B.

95 *See, e.g.*, Big Data Tr. 168–170 (Carol Miaskoff). Disparate impact claims are not permitted under Title II of GINA. *Background Information for EEOC Notice of Proposed Rulemaking on Title II of the Genetic Information Nondiscrimination Act of 2008*, U.S. Equal Emp't Opportunity Comm'n, http://www.eeoc.gov/policy/docs/qanda_geneticinfo.html (last modified May 12, 2009).

96 *See, e.g.*, 29 U.S.C. § 623(a)(1); 42 U. S. C. § 2000e–2(k)(1)(A)(i); 42 U.S.C. § 12112(b)(1); 12 C.F.R. Part 1002 Supp. I § 1002.4(a)–1.

97 *See, e.g.*, Int'l Bhd. of Teamsters v. United States, 431 U.S. 324, 334–35 (1977).

98 *See, e.g.*, Big Data Tr. 168–170 (Carol Miaskoff).

99 *Cf. id.* (explaining how the various equal opportunity laws may apply to big data analytics).

Practices that have a "disparate impact" on protected classes may also violate equal credit or employment opportunity laws.[100] While specific disparate impact standards vary depending on the applicable law, in general, disparate impact occurs when a company employs facially neutral policies or practices that have a disproportionate adverse effect or impact on a protected class,[101] unless those practices or policies further a legitimate business need[102] that cannot reasonably be achieved by means that have less disparate an impact.[103]

Disparate impact analysis has important implications for big data.[104] Under such an analysis, a company that avoids, for example, expressly screening job applicants based on gender and instead uses big data analytics to screen job applicants in a way that has a disparate impact on women may still be subject to certain equal employment opportunity laws, if the screening does not serve a legitimate business need or if the need can reasonably be achieved by another means with a smaller disparate impact.[105] Likewise, if a company makes credit decisions based on zip codes, it may be violating ECOA if the decisions have a disparate impact on a protected class and are not justified by a legitimate business necessity.[106] Even if evidence shows the decisions are justified by a business necessity, if there is a less discriminatory alternative, the decisions may still violate ECOA.[107]

---

[100] *See, e.g.*, 29 U.S.C. § 631(a); 42 U.S.C. § 2000e–2 (k); 42 U.S.C. § 12112(b)(6); 24 C.F.R. § 100.500; 12 C.F.R. Part 1002 Supp. I § 1002.6(a)–2. On June 25, 2015, the Supreme Court in *Texas Department of Housing and Community Affairs v. Inclusive Communities Project, Inc.*, 135 S.Ct. 2507 (2015), held that the disparate impact theory is valid under the FHA.

[101] *See, e.g.*, 12 C.F.R. § 1002.6 (citing Griggs v. Duke Power Co., 401 U.S. 424 (1971), and Albemarle Paper Co. v. Moody, 422 U.S. 405, 430–31 (1975)); 12 C.F.R. Part 1002 Supp. I § 1002.6(a)–2; Policy Statement on Discrimination in Lending, 59 Fed. Reg. 18,266, 18,268 (Apr. 14, 1994).

[102] *See, e.g.*, Tex. Dep't of Cmty. Affairs v. Burdine, 450 U.S. 248, 256–58 (1981); N.Y. City Transit Auth. v. Beazer, 440 U.S. 568, 587 (1979); Zamlen v. City of Cleveland, 906 F.2d 209, 218–20 (6th Cir. 1990); Evans v. City of Evanston, 881 F.2d 382, 383 (7th Cir. 1989); Aguilera v. Cook County Police & Corr. Merit Bd., 760 F.2d 844, 846–47 (7th Cir. 1985). *See also* 12 C.F.R. § 1002.6(a). However, with respect to ADEA cases, the formulation applied by courts is slightly different. *See, e.g.*, Smith v. City of Jackson, 544 U.S. 228, 243 (2005) (holding that the "reasonable factor other than age" test, rather than the business necessity test, is the appropriate standard for determining lawfulness of a practice that disproportionally affects older workers under the ADEA). *See also Questions and Answers on EEOC Final Rule on Disparate Impact and "Reasonable Factors Other Than Age" Under the Age Discrimination Employment Act of 1967*, U.S. Equal Emp't Opportunity Comm'n, http://www.eeoc.gov/laws/regulations/adea_rfoa_qa_final_rule.cfm (last visited on Dec. 28, 2015).

[103] *See, e.g., Albermarle Paper*, 422 U.S. at 425; Int'l Bhd. of Elec. Workers, AFL-CIO, Local Unions Nos. 605 & 985 v. Miss. Power & Light Co., 442 F.3d 313, 318–19 (5th Cir. 2006); Smith v. City of Des Moines, Iowa, 99 F.3d 1466, 1473 (8th Cir. 1996); Contreras v. City of Los Angeles, 656 F.2d 1267, 1285 (9th Cir. 1981); El v. Se. Pa. Transp. Auth., 418 F. Supp. 2d 659, 672 (E.D. Pa. 2005) *aff'd*, 479 F.3d 232 (3d Cir. 2007).

[104] Big data can also facilitate the identification of disparate impact. *See infra* notes 145–47 and accompanying text.

[105] *See, e.g.*, Big Data Tr. 170 (Carol Miaskoff).

[106] The use of zip codes can also raise concerns of redlining, a form of discrimination involving differential treatment on the basis of the race, color, national origin, or other protected characteristic of residents of those areas in which the credit seeker resides, or will reside, or in which residential property to be mortgaged is located. The CFPB and DOJ recently concluded a redlining enforcement action against Hudson City Savings Bank. *See* Complaint, CFPB v. Hudson City Sav. Bank, No. 15-07056 (D.N.J. Sept. 24, 2015), http://files.consumerfinance.gov/f/201509_cfpb_hudson-city-joint-complaint.pdf. *See also* Consumer Fin. Protection Bureau, CFPB Examination Procedures: ECOA Baseline Review Modules 16–18 (2013), http://files.consumerfinance.gov/f/201307_cfpb_ecoa_baseline-review-module-fair-lending.pdf.

[107] The examples above are illustrative and do not necessarily provide an exhaustive list of all ways that big data could have a disparate impact on consumers.

The FTC's enforcement actions include dozens of consent orders resolving alleged violations of ECOA. Some of these cases have been based on a disparate treatment theory. For example, ECOA prohibits discrimination against applicants who are receiving public assistance.[108] The Commission has brought cases against lenders that allegedly excluded public assistance income in deciding whether to extend credit.[109] Likewise, ECOA prohibits discounting or refusing to consider income on the basis of marital status.[110] The FTC has brought cases against lenders that allegedly failed to aggregate the income of unmarried joint applicants, while combining incomes for applicants who were married.[111]

The FTC also has alleged discrimination under a disparate impact legal standard under ECOA. For example, the FTC settled two cases alleging that lenders failed to appropriately monitor loan officers whose mortgage loans resulted in minority applicants' being charged higher prices than non-Latino white applicants.[112] The Commission alleged that the statistically significant pricing disparities could not be explained by any legitimate underwriting risk factors or credit characteristics of the applicants.

Workshop discussions focused in particular on whether advertising could implicate equal opportunity laws.[113] For example, suppose big data analytics show that single women are more likely to apply for subprime credit products. Would targeting advertisements for these products to single women violate ECOA?[114] Certainly, prohibiting single women from applying for a prime credit card based on their marital status would violate ECOA.[115] But what if a single woman would qualify for the prime product, but because of big data analytics, the subprime product with a higher interest rate is the only one advertised to her?

In most cases, a company's advertisement to a particular community for a credit offer that is open to all to apply is unlikely, by itself, to violate ECOA, absent disparate treatment or an unjustified disparate

---

108 15 U.S.C. § 1691(a)(2).

109 *See, e.g.*, Complaint, United States v. Franklin Acceptance Corp., No. 99-cv-2435 (E.D. Penn. filed May 13, 1999), https://www.ftc.gov/sites/default/files/documents/cases/1999/05/franklincmp.htm.

110 15 U.S.C. § 1691(a)(1).

111 *See, e.g.*, Complaint, United States v. Ford Motor Credit Co., No. 99-cv-57887 (GEW) (E.D. Mich. filed Dec. 9, 1999), https://www.ftc.gov/sites/default/files/documents/cases/1999/12/fordmotorcompanyfederalcourtcomplaint.pdf.

112 *See* Complaint, FTC v. Gateway Diversified Funding Mortg. Servs., No. 08-5805 (E.D. Pa. filed Dec. 16, 2008), https://www.ftc.gov/sites/default/files/documents/cases/2008/12/081216gatewaycmpt.pdf; Complaint, FTC v. Golden Empire Mortgage, Inc., No. 09-03227 CAS(SHx) (C.D. Cal. filed May 7, 2009), https://www.ftc.gov/sites/default/files/documents/cases/2009/05/090511gemcmpt.pdf.

113 *See, e.g.*, Big Data Tr. 179–83 (Peter Swire), 187–90 (Peter Swire, Leonard Chanin, and C. Lee Peeler in conversation), 204–05 (Peter Swire), 268–69 (Christopher Calabrese).

114 In the context of mortgage advertising, creditors should also consider the FHA. 42 U.S.C. §§ 3601–3631; 24 C.F.R. Parts 100, 103, and 104. Regulations that implement the FHA prohibit "[f]ailing or refusing to provide to any person information regarding the availability of loans or other financial assistance, application requirements, procedures or standards for the review and approval of loans or financial assistance, or providing information which is inaccurate or different from that provided others, because of race, color, religion, sex, handicap, familial status, or national origin." 24 C.F.R. § 100.120(b)(1).

115 15 U.S.C. § 1691(a)(1).

impact in subsequent lending.[116] Nevertheless, companies should proceed with caution in this area. In credit transactions,[117] Regulation B, which is the implementing regulation for ECOA, prohibits creditors[118] from making oral or written statements, in advertising or otherwise, to applicants or prospective applicants that would discourage on a prohibited basis a reasonable person from making or pursuing an application.[119] With respect to prescreened solicitations, Regulation B also requires creditors to maintain records of the solicitations and the criteria used to select potential recipients.[120] Advertising and marketing practices could impact a creditor's subsequent lending patterns and the terms and conditions of the credit received by borrowers, even if credit offers are open to all who apply. In some cases, the DOJ has cited a creditor's advertising choices as evidence of discrimination.[121]

Ultimately, as with the FCRA, the question of whether a practice is unlawful under equal opportunity laws is a case-specific inquiry. Accordingly, companies should proceed with caution if their practices could suggest disparate treatment or have a demonstrable disparate impact based on protected characteristics.

3. The Federal Trade Commission Act

Section 5 of the Federal Trade Commission Act ("Section 5") prohibits unfair or deceptive acts or practices in or affecting commerce.[122] Unlike the FCRA or equal opportunity laws, Section 5 is not confined to particular market sectors but is generally applicable to most companies acting in commerce.[123] Under Section 5, an act or practice is *deceptive* if it involves a material statement or omission that is likely to mislead a consumer acting reasonably under the circumstances.[124] For example, if a company violates a material promise—whether that

---

116 *See, e.g.*, Big Data Tr. 178–191 (Peter Swire, C. Lee Peeler, and Leonard Chanin in conversation).

117 Under Regulation B, credit transaction means "every aspect of an applicant's dealings with a creditor regarding an application for credit or an existing extension of credit (including, but not limited to, information requirements; investigation procedures; standards of creditworthiness; terms of credit; furnishing of credit information; revocation, alteration, or termination of credit; and collection procedures)." 12 C.F.R. § 1002.2(m).

118 Under Regulation B, a creditor "does not include a person whose only participation in a credit transaction involves honoring a credit card." *Id.* § 1002.2(l).

119 *Id.* § 1002.4(b).

120 *Id.* § 1002.12(b)(7).

121 *See, e.g.*, Complaint, United States v. First United Sec. Bank, No. 1 09-cv-00644 (S.D. Ala. filed Sept. 30, 2009), http://www.justice.gov/sites/default/files/crt/legacy/2010/12/14/fusbcomp.pdf.

122 15 U.S.C. § 45(a)(1) (2012).

123 The FTC's consumer protection mandate is broad. Under Section 5 of the FTC Act, 15 U.S.C. § 45, the Commission has the power to prevent "persons, partnerships, and corporations" from using unfair or deceptive acts or practices in or affecting commerce, with certain limited exceptions. Those exceptions include: (1) banks and savings and loan institutions as described in 15 U.S.C. § 57a(f)(2) and (3); (2) federal credit unions as described in 15 U.S.C. § 57a(f)(4); (3) common carrier activities subject to subtitle IV of title 49 and the Communications Act of 1934; and (4) air carriers and foreign air carriers.

124 FTC Policy Statement on Deception, 103 F.T.C. 110, 174 (1984) (appended to Cliffdale Assocs., Inc., 103 F.T.C. 110, 174 (1984)). *See also* POM Wonderful LLC, No. C-9344, 2013 WL 268926, at *18 (F.T.C. Jan. 16, 2013).

promise is to refrain from sharing data with third parties,[125] to provide consumers choices about sharing,[126] or to safeguard consumers' personal information[127]—it will likely be engaged in a deceptive practice under Section 5.

Likewise, a failure to disclose material information may violate Section 5. In *CompuCredit*, for instance, the FTC included an allegation in the complaint that although a credit card marketing company touted the ability of consumers to use the card for cash advances, it deceptively failed to disclose that, based on a behavioral scoring model, consumers' credit lines would be reduced if they used their cards for such cash advances or if they used their cards for certain types of transactions, including marriage counseling, bars and nightclubs, pawn shops, and massage parlors.[128] Among other things, the settlement prohibits CompuCredit from making misrepresentations to consumers in the marketing of credit cards, including misrepresentations about the amount of available credit.[129]

In addition, under Section 5, an act or practice is *unfair* if it is likely to cause substantial consumer injury, the injury is not reasonably avoidable by consumers, and the injury is not outweighed by benefits to consumers or competition.[130] One example of a potentially unfair practice is the failure to reasonably secure consumers' data where that failure is likely to cause substantial injury.[131] Companies that maintain big data on consumers should take care to reasonably secure that data commensurate with the amount and sensitivity

---

125 *See, e.g.*, Goldenshores Techs., LLC, No. C-4446 (F.T.C. Mar. 31, 2014), https://www.ftc.gov/system/files/documents/cases/140409goldenshoresdo.pdf; FTC v. Myspace LLC, No. C-4369 (F.T.C. Aug. 30, 2012), https://www.ftc.gov/sites/default/files/documents/cases/2012/09/120911myspacedo.pdf.

126 *See, e.g.*, Compete, Inc., No. D-4384 (F.T.C. Feb. 20, 2013), https://www.ftc.gov/sites/default/files/documents/cases/2013/02/130222competedo.pdf; United States v. Path, Inc., No. C-13-0448 (N.D. Cal. Feb. 8, 2013), https://www.ftc.gov/sites/default/files/documents/cases/2013/02/130201pathincdo.pdf; Google Inc., No. C-4336 (F.T.C. Oct. 13, 2011), https://www.ftc.gov/sites/default/files/documents/cases/2011/10/111024googlebuzzdo.pdf; Facebook, Inc., No. C-4365 (F.T.C. July 27, 2012), https://www.ftc.gov/sites/default/files/documents/cases/2012/08/120810facebookdo.pdf; Chitika, Inc., No. C-4324 (F.T.C. June 7, 2011), https://www.ftc.gov/sites/default/files/documents/cases/2011/06/110617chitikado.pdf.

127 *See, e.g.*, Snapchat, Inc., C-4501 (F.T.C. Dec. 23, 2014), https://www.ftc.gov/system/files/documents/cases/141231snapchatdo.pdf; Fandango, LLC, No. C-4481 (F.T.C. Aug. 13, 2014), https://www.ftc.gov/system/files/documents/cases/140819fandangodo.pdf; Credit Karma, Inc., C-4480 (F.T.C. Aug. 13, 2014), https://www.ftc.gov/system/files/documents/cases/1408creditkarmado.pdf; Twitter, Inc., No. C-4316 (F.T.C. Mar. 2, 2011), https://www.ftc.gov/sites/default/files/documents/cases/2011/03/110311twitterdo.pdf; Reed Elsevier Inc., No. C-4226 (F.T.C. July 29, 2008), https://www.ftc.gov/sites/default/files/documents/cases/2008/08/080801reeddo.pdf.

128 Complaint, *CompuCredit*, No. 1:08-cv-1976-BBM-RGV (N.D. Ga. filed June 10, 2008), https://www.ftc.gov/sites/default/files/documents/cases/2008/06/080610compucreditcmplt.pdf.

129 *Id.*

130 15 U.S.C. § 45(n) (2012). *See also* FTC Policy Statement on Unfairness (appended to Int'l Harvester Co., 104 F.T.C. 949, 1070 (1984)).

131 *See, e.g.*, GMR Transcription Servs., Inc., No. C-4482 (F.T.C. Aug. 14, 2014), https://www.ftc.gov/system/files/documents/cases/140821gmrdo.pdf; GeneWize Life Scis., Inc., No. C-4457 (F.T.C. May 8, 2014), https://www.ftc.gov/system/files/documents/cases/140512foruintdo.pdf; HTC Am., Inc., No. C-4406 (F.T.C. June 25, 2013), https://www.ftc.gov/sites/default/files/documents/cases/2013/07/130702htcdo.pdf; *Compete*, No. C-4384 (F.T.C. Feb. 20, 2013), https://www.ftc.gov/sites/default/files/documents/cases/2013/02/130222competedo.pdf; Upromise, Inc., No. C-4351 (F.T.C. Mar. 27, 2012), https://www.ftc.gov/sites/default/files/documents/cases/2012/04/120403upromisedo.pdf.

of the data at issue, the size and complexity of the company's operations, and the cost of available security measures.[132] For example, a company that maintains Social Security numbers or medical information about individual consumers should have particularly robust security measures as compared to a company that maintains consumers' names only.

Another example of a potentially unfair practice that the Commission has challenged is the sale of data to customers that a company knows or has reason to know will use the data for fraudulent purposes. The Commission's cases against Sequoia One and ChoicePoint are instructive in this regard. In *Sequoia One*, the FTC's complaint alleges that the company sold the personal information of financially distressed payday loan applicants—including Social Security numbers, financial account numbers, and bank routing numbers—to non-lender third-parties and one of these third parties used the information to withdraw millions of dollars from consumers' accounts without their authorization.[133]

In *ChoicePoint*, the Commission alleged that the company sold the personal information of more than 163,000 consumers to identity thieves posing as legitimate subscribers, despite obvious red flags that should have alerted the company to the potential fraud.[134] As these cases show, at a minimum, companies must not sell their big data analytics products to customers if they know or have reason to know that those customers will use the products for fraudulent purposes.

Section 5 may also apply under similar circumstances if products are sold to customers that use the products for discriminatory purposes.[135] The inquiry will be fact-specific, and in every case, the test will be whether the company is offering or using big data analytics in a deceptive or unfair way.

---

132 *See generally* FED. TRADE COMM'N, START WITH SECURITY: A GUIDE FOR BUSINESS (2015), https://www.ftc.gov/system/files/documents/plain-language/pdf0205-startwithsecurity.pdf.

133 FTC v. Sequoia One, LLC, No. 2:15-cv-01512 (D. Nev. Aug. 10, 2015), https://www.ftc.gov/system/files/documents/cases/150812sequoiaonemcdonnellstip.pdf; Complaint, *Sequoia One*, No. 2-15-cv-01512 (D. Nev. filed Aug. 7, 2015), https://www.ftc.gov/system/files/documents/cases/150812sequoiaonecmpt.pdf. *See also* Press Release, Fed. Trade Comm'n, FTC Charges Data Broker with Facilitating the Theft of Millions of Dollars from Consumers' Accounts (Dec. 23, 2014), https://www.ftc.gov/news-events/press-releases/2014/12/ftc-charges-data-broker-facilitating-theft-millions-dollars. In *LeapLab*, the Commission's complaint alleges that the company bought payday loan applications of financially strapped consumers, and then sold that information—including Social Security numbers and financial account numbers—to marketers whom it knew had no legitimate need for it. Complaint at 5–10, LeapLab, LLC, No. 2:14-cv-02750 (D. Ariz. filed Dec. 22, 2014), https://www.ftc.gov/system/files/documents/cases/141223leaplabcmpt.pdf. One of these marketers allegedly used the information to withdraw millions of dollars from consumers' accounts without their authorization. *Id.* at 9–10.

134 United States v. ChoicePoint, Inc., No. 1:06-cv-0198-JTC (N.D. Ga. Feb. 15, 2006), https://www.ftc.gov/sites/default/files/documents/cases/2006/01/stipfinaljudgement.pdf.

135 *Cf.* DATA BROKERS REPORT, *supra* note 7, at 56.

Questions for Legal Compliance

In light of these existing laws, companies already using or considering engaging in big data analytics should, among other things, consider the following:

- If you compile big data for others who will use it for eligibility decisions (such as credit, employment, insurance, housing, government benefits, and the like), are you complying with the accuracy and privacy provisions of the FCRA? FCRA requirements include requirements to (1) have reasonable procedures in place to ensure the maximum possible accuracy of the information you provide, (2) provide notices to users of your reports, (3) allow consumers to access information you have about them, and (4) allow consumers to correct inaccuracies.

- If you receive big data products from another entity that you will use for eligibility decisions, are you complying with the provisions applicable to users of consumer reports? For example, the FCRA requires that entities that use this information for employment purposes certify that they have a "permissible purpose" to obtain it, certify that they will not use it in a way that violates equal opportunity laws, provide pre-adverse action notice to consumers, and thereafter provide adverse action notices to those same consumers.

- If you are a creditor using big data analytics in a credit transaction, are you complying with the requirement to provide statements of specific reasons for adverse action under ECOA? Are you complying with ECOA requirements related to requests for information and record retention?

- If you use big data analytics in a way that might adversely affect people in their ability to obtain credit, housing, or employment:

  - Are you treating people differently based on a prohibited basis, such as race or national origin?

  - Do your policies, practices, or decisions have an adverse effect or impact on a member of a protected class, and if they do, are they justified by a legitimate business need that cannot reasonably be achieved by means that are less disparate in their impact?

- Are you honoring promises you make to consumers and providing consumers material information about your data practices?

- Are you maintaining reasonable security over consumer data?

- Are you undertaking reasonable measures to know the purposes for which your customers are using your data?

  - If you know that your customer will use your big data products to commit fraud, do not sell your products to that customer. If you have reason to believe that your data will be used to commit fraud, ask more specific questions about how your data will be used.

  - If you know that your customer will use your big data products for discriminatory purposes, do not sell your products to that customer. If you have reason to believe that your data will be used for discriminatory purposes, ask more specific questions about how your data will be used.

B. Special Policy Considerations Raised by Big Data Research

Workshop and seminar panelists, academics, and others have also engaged in important research in the field of big data.[136] Some of this research has focused on how big data analytics could negatively affect low-income and underserved populations.[137] Researchers note there is a potential for incorporating errors and biases at every stage, from choosing the data set used to make predictions, to defining the problem to be addressed through big data, to making decisions based on the results of big data analysis.[138] While having the ability to use more data can increase the power of the analysis, simply adding more data does not necessarily correct inaccuracies or remove biases. In addition, the complexity of the data and statistical models can make it difficult for analysts to fully understand and explain the underlying model or its results. Even when data analysts are very careful, the results of their analysis may affect particular sets of individuals differently because their models may use variables that turn out to operate no differently than proxies for protected classes.[139] Or researchers may simply lack information that would allow them to determine whether their results have such effects. Numerous researchers and commenters discuss how big data could be used in the future to the disadvantage of low-income and underserved communities and adversely affect consumers on the basis of legally protected characteristics in hiring, housing, lending, and other processes.[140]

---

136 *See generally* Robinson + Yu Comment #00080, *supra* note 53; Ctr. for Data Innovation Comment #00055, *supra* note 8; Comment #00042 from Peter Swire, Ga. Inst. of Tech. & Future of Privacy Forum, to Fed. Trade Comm'n (Sept. 15, 2014), https://www.ftc.gov/system/files/documents/public_comments/2014/09/00042-92638.pdf; Future of Privacy Forum Comment #00027, *supra* note 23; Ctr. on Privacy & Tech. at Geo. L. Comment #00024, *supra* note 8; Nat'l Consumer L. Ctr. Comment #00018, *supra* note 1; N.Y.U. Info. L. Inst. Comment #00015, *supra* note 8; World Privacy Forum Comment #00014, *supra* note 19; Tech. Pol'y Inst. Comment #00010, *supra* note 8; Ctr. for Dig. Democracy & U.S. PIRG Educ. Fund Comment #00003, *supra* note 8.

137 *See, e.g.*, Solon Barocas & Andrew Selbst, *Big Data's Disparate Impact*, 104 Cal. Law R. _ (forthcoming 2016), http://papers.ssrn.com/sol3/papers.cfm?abstract_id=2477899##; Alex Rosenblat et al., *Networked Employment Discrimination*, (Data & Society Research Inst., Working Paper Oct. 8, 2014), http://www.datasociety.net/pubs/fow/EmploymentDiscrimination.pdf; Gary Marcus & Ernest Davis, *Eight (No, Nine!) Problems With Big Data*, N.Y. Times (Apr. 6, 2014), http://www.nytimes.com/2014/04/07/opinion/eight-no-nine-problems-with-big-data.html?_r=0; Tim Harford, *Big Data: Are We Making a Big Mistake?*, FT Magazine (Mar. 28, 2014), http://www.ft.com/intl/cms/s/2/21a6c7d8-b479-11e3-a09a-00144feabdc0.html. *See generally* Joseph Turow, The Daily You: How the New Advertising Industry is Defining Your Identity and Your Worth (2012).

138 *See, e.g.*, Big Data Tr. 19–25 (Solon Barocas). *See also* Nat'l Consumer L. Ctr. Comment #00018, *supra* note 1, at 14–15; World Privacy Forum Comment #00014, *supra* note 19, at 6–17. *See generally* Barocas & Selbst, *supra* note 137.

139 Barocas & Selbst, *supra* note 137, at 20–22. Researchers note that data mining poses the additional problem of giving data miners the ability to disguise intentional discrimination as unintentional. *Id.* at 22–23. *See also* Paul Ohm, *Changing the Rules: General Principles for Data Use and Analysis*, in Privacy, Big Data, and the Public Good: Frameworks for Engagement 100–02 (Julia Lane et al. eds., 2014). For examples of the kinds of analyses that can be conducted to detect whether model variables are proxies for protected characteristics, see generally Fed. Trade Comm'n, Credit-Based Insurance Scores: Impacts on Consumers of Automobile Insurance (2007), http://www.ftc.gov/sites/default/files/documents/reports/credit-based-insurance-scores-impacts-consumers-automobile-insurance-report-congress-federal-trade/p044804facta_report_credit-based_insurance_scores.pdf, and Bd. of Governors of the Fed. Reserve Sys., Report to Congress on Credit Scoring and Its Effects on the Availability and Affordability of Credit (2007), http://www.federalreserve.gov/boarddocs/rptcongress/creditscore/creditscore.pdf.

140 *See generally* Robinson + Yu Comment #00080, *supra* note 53; Am.'s Open Tech. Inst. Comment #00078, *supra* note 46; Ctr. for Democracy & Tech. Comment #00075, *supra* note 61; Am. Civil Liberties Union Comment #00059, *supra* note 61; Ctr. on Privacy & Tech. at Geo. L. Comment #00024, *supra* note 8; Nat'l Consumer L. Ctr. Comment #00018, *supra* note 1;

On the other hand, several stakeholders argue that these concerns are overstated.[141] Some emphasize that, to the extent the various steps in data mining lead to disparate impact, these issues are not new—they are inherent in any statistical analysis.[142] Other writers note that, rather than disadvantaging minorities in the hiring process, big data can help to create "a labor market that's fairer to people at every stage of their careers."[143] For example, companies can use big data algorithms to find employees from within underrepresented segments of the population.[144] They can also use big data to identify biases so that they can choose candidates based on merit rather than using mechanisms that depend on the reviewers' biases.[145] Furthermore, as other stakeholders have noted, big data can help "reduce the rate of 'false positive' cases that potentially make disparate treatment a problem"[146] and can help identify whether correlations exist between prices and variables such as race, gender or ethnicity.[147] These stakeholders do not argue that we should ignore discrimination where it occurs; rather, they argue that we should recognize the potential benefits of big data to reduce discriminatory harm.

Common Sense Media Comment #00016, *supra* note 8; N.Y.U. Info. L. Inst. Comment #00015, *supra* note 8; World Privacy Forum Comment #00014, *supra* note 19; Ctr. for Dig. Democracy & U.S. PIRG Educ. Fund Comment #00003, *supra* note 8. *See also* Barocas & Selbst, *supra* note 137; Crawford, *supra* note 39.

141 *See, e.g.*, Big Data Tr. 75 (Gene Gsell). *See generally* Comment #00081 from Berin Szoka & Tom Struble, TechFreedom, & Geoffrey Manne & Ben Sperry, Int'l Ctr. for L. & Econ., to Fed. Trade Comm'n (Nov. 3, 2014), https://www.ftc.gov/system/files/documents/public_comments/2014/11/00081-92956.pdf; Comment #00074 from Howard Fienberg, Mktg. Research Assoc., to Fed. Trade Comm'n (Oct. 31, 2014), https://www.ftc.gov/system/files/documents/public_comments/2014/10/00074-92927.pdf; Comment #00070 from Bijan Madhani, Computer & Commc'ns Indus. Assoc., to Fed. Trade Comm'n (Oct. 31, 2014), https://www.ftc.gov/system/files/documents/public_comments/2014/10/00070-92912.pdf; NetChoice Comment #00066, *supra* note 23; Ctr. for Data Innovation Comment #00055, *supra* note 8; Ctr. for Data Innovation Comment #00026, *supra* note 8; Tech. Pol'y Inst. Comment #00010, *supra* note 8; Viktor Mayer-Schonberger & Kenneth Cukier, Big Data: A Revolution That Will Transform How We Live, Work, And Think (2013).

142 *See, e.g.*, Dan Gray, *Ethics, Privacy and Discrimination in the Age of Big Data*, Dataconomy (Dec. 3, 2014), http://dataconomy.com/ethics-privacy-and-discrimination-in-the-age-of-big-data/. *But see* Jeff Leek, *Why Big Data Is in Trouble: They Forgot About Applied Statistics*, SimplyStats (May 7, 2014), http://simplystatistics.org/2014/05/07/why-big-data-is-in-trouble-they-forgot-about-applied-statistics/ (noting that big data users have not given sufficient attention to issues that statisticians have been thinking about for a long time: sampling populations, multiple testing, bias, and overfitting).

143 *See, e.g.*, Don Peck, *They're Watching You at Work*, Atlantic (Dec. 2013), http://www.theatlantic.com/magazine/archive/2013/12/theyre-watching-you-at-work/354681/.

144 *See, e.g.*, Big Data Tr. 126 (Mark MacCarthy), 251 (Christopher Wolf). *See also* Software & Info. Indus. Assoc. Comment #00067, *supra* note 2, at 7; Future of Privacy Forum Comment #00027, *supra* note 23, attached report entitled, Big Data: A Tool for Fighting Discrimination and Empowering Groups, at 1–2.

145 *See, e.g.*, Anne Loehr, *Big Data for HR: Can Predictive Analytics Help Decrease Discrimination in the Workplace?*, Huffington Post (Mar. 23, 2015), http://www.huffingtonpost.com/anne-loehr/big-data-for-hr-can-predi_b_6905754.html.

146 White House Feb. 2015 Report, *supra* note 56, at 16.

147 *Id.* at 17. Economists have documented ways that data can help identify discrimination against protected groups in a wide variety of settings. For example, a randomized experiment changed the names on resumes sent to employers from white-sounding names to African-American sounding names; resumes with white-sounding names were 50 percent more likely to be called back for an interview. Marianne Bertrand & Sendhil Mullainathan, *Are Emily and Greg More Employable Than Lakisha and Jamal? A Field Experiment on Labor Market Discrimination*, 94 Am. Econ. Rev. 991, 991–1013 (2004). Research from the early days of the Internet found that African-Americans and Latinos paid about 2 percent more for used cars purchased offline, but paid similar prices for those purchased online; the proffered reason was that individuals were anonymous online. Fiona Scott Morton et al., *Consumer Information and Discrimination: Does the Internet Affect the Pricing of New Cars to Women and Minorities?*, 1 Quantitative Mktg. & Econs. 65, 65–92 (2003). *See also* Devin Pope & Justin Sydnor, *Implementing Anti-Discrimination Policies in Statistical Profiling Models*, 3 Am. Econ. J.: Econ. Pol'y 206, 206–231 (2011), http://faculty.chicagobooth.edu/devin.pope/research/pdf/Website_Antidiscrimination%20Models.pdf.

Collectively, this research suggests that big data offers both new potential discriminatory harms and new potential solutions to discriminatory harms. To maximize the benefits and limit the harms, companies should consider the questions raised by research in this area. These questions include the following:

1. **How representative is your data set?**

Workshop participants and researchers note that the data sets, on which all big data analysis relies, may be missing information about certain populations, e.g., individuals who are more careful about revealing information about themselves, who are less involved in the formal economy, who have unequal access or less fluency in technology resulting in a digital divide[148] or data desert,[149] or whose behaviors are simply not observed because they are believed to be less profitable constituencies.[150]

Recent examples demonstrate the impact of missing information about particular populations on data analytics. For example, Hurricane Sandy generated more than twenty million tweets between October 27 and November 1, 2012.[151] If organizations were to use this data to determine where services should be deployed, the people who needed services the most may not have received them. The greatest number of tweets about Hurricane Sandy came from Manhattan, creating the illusion that Manhattan was the hub of the disaster. Very few messages originated from more severely affected locations, such as Breezy Point, Coney Island, and Rockaway—areas with lower levels of smartphone ownership and Twitter usage. As extended power blackouts drained batteries and limited cellular access, even fewer tweets came from the worst hit areas. As one researcher noted, "data are assumed to accurately reflect the social world, but there are significant gaps, with little or no signal coming from particular communities."[152]

Organizations have developed ways to overcome this issue. For example, the city of Boston developed an application called Street Bump that utilizes smartphone features such as GPS feeds to collect and report to the city information about road conditions, including potholes. However, after the release of the application, the Street Bump team recognized that because lower income individuals may be less likely to carry smartphones, the data was likely not fully representative of all road conditions. If the city had

---

148 A digital divide refers to the fact that certain populations may not have access to the Internet. *See, e.g.*, Ctr. for Data Innovation Comment #00055, *supra* note 8, at 2; Nat'l Consumer L. Ctr. Comment #00018, *supra* note 1, at 9, 27; Ctr. for Dig. Democracy & U.S. PIRG Educ. Fund Comment #00003, *supra* note 8, at 2.

149 Data deserts are geographic "areas characterized by a lack of access to high-quality data that may be used to generate social and economic benefits." Ctr. for Data Innovation, Comment #00055, *supra* note 8, at 3. "[I]f some communities are not represented in the data, decisions may overlook members of these communities and their unique needs." *Id.*, attached report entitled, Wikipedia Edits Reveal America's Data Deserts, at 1.

150 *See, e.g.*, Big Data Tr. 100–02 (Dr. Nicol Turner-Lee), 256–58 (Daniel Castro). *See also* Ctr. for Dig. Democracy & U.S. PIRG Educ. Fund Comment #00003, *supra* note 8, at 2; Quentin Hardy, *Why Big Data Is Not Truth*, N.Y. Times (June 1, 2013), http://bits.blogs.nytimes.com/2013/06/01/why-big-data-is-not-truth/?_php=true&_type=blogs&_r=1 (reviewing a speech provided by Kate Crawford); danah boyd & Kate Crawford, *Critical Questions for Big Data*, 15 Info., Comm'n & Soc'y 662, 668–70 (2012), http://dx.doi.org/10.1080/1369118X.2012.678878.

151 *See, e.g.*, Crawford, *supra* note 39. *See also* Grinberg et al., *supra* note 37.

152 Crawford, *supra* note 39.

continued relying on the biased data, it might have skewed road services to higher income neighborhoods. The team addressed this problem by issuing its application to city workers who service the whole city and supplementing the data with that from the public.[153] This example demonstrates why it is important to consider the digital divide and other issues of underrepresentation and overrepresentation in data inputs before launching a product or service in order to avoid skewed and potentially unfair ramifications.

2. Does your data model account for biases?

While large data sets can give insight into previously intractable challenges, hidden biases at both the collection and analytics stages of big data's life cycle could lead to disparate impact.[154] Researchers have noted that big data analytics "can reproduce existing patterns of discrimination, inherit the prejudice of prior decision-makers, or simply reflect the widespread biases that persist in society."[155] For example, if an employer uses big data analytics to synthesize information gathered on successful existing employees to define a "good employee candidate," the employer could risk incorporating previous discrimination in employment decisions into new employment decisions.[156] Even prior to the widespread use of big data, there is some evidence of the use of data leading to the reproduction of existing biases. For example, one researcher has noted that a hospital developed a computer model to help identify "good medical school applicants" based on performance levels of previous and existing students, but, in doing so, the model reproduced prejudices in prior admission decisions.[157]

Companies can also design big data algorithms that learn from human behavior; these algorithms may "learn" to generate biased results. For example, one academic found that Reuters and Google queries for names identified by researchers to be associated with African-Americans were more likely to return advertisements for arrest records than for names identified by researchers to be associated with white Americans.[158] The academic concluded that determining why this discrimination was occurring was beyond the scope of her research, but reasoned that search engines' algorithms may learn to prioritize arrest record ads for searches of names associated with African-Americans if people click on such ads more frequently than other ads.[159] This could reinforce the display of such ads and perpetuate the cycle.

---

153 *See, e.g.*, Big Data Tr. 21–22 (Solon Barocas), 259–60 (Michael Spadea). *See also* Tech. Pol'y Inst. Comment #00010, *supra* note 8, at 4 & attached report at 15; WHITE HOUSE MAY 2014 REPORT, *supra* note 1, at 51–52.

154 *See, e.g.*, Big Data Tr. 19–25 (Solon Barocas), 40–41 (Joseph Turow).

155 Barocas & Selbst, *supra* note 137, at 3–4.

156 *See, e.g.*, Big Data Tr. 168–70 (Carol Miaskoff). *Cf.* Barocas & Selbst, *supra* note 137, at 9–11.

157 *See generally* Stella Lowry & Gordon Macpherson, *A Blot on the Profession*, 296 BRITISH MED. J., 657, 657–58 (1988), http://www.ncbi.nlm.nih.gov/pmc/articles/PMC2545288/pdf/bmj00275-0003.pdf.

158 *See generally* Latanya Sweeney, *Discrimination in Online Ad Delivery*, 56 COMMC'NS OF THE ACM 44 (2013), http://papers.ssrn.com/sol3/papers.cfm?abstract_id=2208240&download=yes. *See also* Big Data Tr. 64–65 (David Robinson); Robinson + Yu Comment #00080, *supra* note 53, at 16–17; N.Y.U. Info. L. Inst. Comment #00015, *supra* note 8, at 6.

159 Sweeney, *supra* note 158, at 34. *See also* Bianca Bosker, *Google's Online Ad Results Guilty of Racial Profiling, According to New Study*, HUFFINGTON POST (Feb. 5, 2013), http://www.huffingtonpost.com/2013/02/05/online-

Companies should therefore think carefully about how the data sets and the algorithms they use have been generated. Indeed, if they identify potential biases in the creation of these data sets or the algorithms, companies should develop strategies to overcome them. As noted above, Google changed its interview and hiring process to ask more behavioral questions and to focus less on academic grades after discovering that replicating its existing definitions of a "good employee" was resulting in a homogeneous tech workforce.[160] More broadly, companies are starting to recognize that if their big data algorithms only consider applicants from "top tier" colleges to help them make hiring decisions, they may be incorporating previous biases in college admission decisions.[161] As in the examples discussed above, companies should develop ways to use big data to expand the pool of qualified applicants they will consider.[162]

3. How accurate are your predictions based on big data?

Some researchers have also found that big data analysis does not give sufficient attention to traditional applied statistics issues, thus leading to incorrect results and predictions.[163] They note that while big data is very good at detecting correlations, it does not explain which correlations are meaningful.[164]

A prime example that demonstrates the limitations of big data analytics is Google Flu Trends, a machine-learning algorithm for predicting the number of flu cases based on Google search terms. To predict the spread of influenza across the United States, the Google team analyzed the top fifty million search terms for indications that the flu had broken out in particular locations. While, at first, the algorithms appeared to create accurate predictions of where the flu was more prevalent, it generated highly inaccurate estimates over time.[165] This could be because the algorithm failed to take into account certain variables. For example, the algorithm may not have taken into account that people would be more likely to search for flu-related terms if the local news ran a story on a flu outbreak, even if the outbreak occurred halfway around the world. As one researcher has noted, Google Flu Trends demonstrates that a "theory-free analysis of mere correlations is inevitably fragile.

---

racial-profiling_n_2622556.html ("[O]ver time, as certain templates are clicked more frequently than others, Google will attempt to optimize its customer's ad by more frequently showing the ad that garners the most clicks.").

160 *See supra* notes 35–36 and accompanying text. *See also* Am.'s Open Tech. Inst. Comment #00078, *supra* note 46, at 60–61.

161 *Cf.* Matt Richtel, *How Big Data Is Playing Recruiter for Specialized Workers*, N.Y. Times (Apr. 27, 2013), http://www.nytimes.com/2013/04/28/technology/how-big-data-is-playing-recruiter-for-specialized-workers.html (noting that some companies are using technology to find candidates based on their ability to succeed on the job rather than traditional markers, such as a degree from a top college).

162 The Commission recognizes that, to address data sets that incorporate previous prejudices, companies may need to collect demographic information about consumers that they would not otherwise collect. If they do collect this information, they should provide disclosures and choices to consumers where appropriate.

163 *See, e.g.*, David Lazer et al., *The Parable of Google Flu: Traps in Big Data Analysis*, 343 Sci. 1203, 1203–05 (2014), http://gking.harvard.edu/files/gking/files/0314policyforumff.pdf; Marcus & Davis, *supra* note 137; Steve Lohr, *Google Flu Trends: The Limits of Big Data*, N.Y. Times (Mar. 28, 2014), http://bits.blogs.nytimes.com/2014/03/28/google-flu-trends-the-limits-of-big-data/?_r=0.

164 *See, e.g.*, Marcus & Davis, *supra* note 137. Likewise, these researchers note that whenever the source of information for a big data analysis is itself a product of big data, opportunities for reinforcing errors exist. *See id.*

165 *See supra* note 163 and accompanying text. *Cf.* Tech. Pol'y Inst. Comment #00010, *supra* note 8, attached report at 5–6.

If you have no idea what is behind a correlation, you have no idea what might cause that correlation to break down."[166]

As another example, workshop participants discussed the fact that lenders can improve access to credit by using non-traditional indicators, e.g., rental or utility bill payment history.[167] Consumers, however, have the right to withhold rent if their landlord does not provide heat or basic sanitation services. In these instances, simply compiling rental payment history would not necessarily demonstrate whether the person is a good credit risk.[168]

In some cases, these sources of inaccuracies are unlikely to have significant negative effects on consumers. For example, it may be that big data analytics shows that 30 percent of consumers who buy diapers will respond to an ad for baby formula. That response rate may be enough for a marketer to find it worthwhile to send buyers of diapers an advertisement for baby formula. The 70 percent of consumers who buy diapers but are not interested in formula can disregard the ad or discard it at little cost. Similarly, consumers who are interested in formula and who do not buy diapers are unlikely to be substantially harmed because they did not get the ad.

On the other hand, if big data analytics are used as the basis for access to credit, housing, or other similar benefits, the potential effects on consumers from inaccuracies could be substantial.[169] For example, suppose big data analytics predict that people who do not participate in social media are 30 percent more likely to be identity thieves, leading a fraud detection tool to flag such people as "risky." Suppose further that a wireless company uses this tool and requires "risky" people to submit additional documentation before they can obtain a cell phone contract. These people may not be able to obtain the contract if they do not have the required documentation. And they may never know why they were denied the ability to complete

---

166 Harford, *supra* note 137, at 133.

167 *See, e.g.*, Big Data Tr. 51–52 (David Robinson), 83–84 (Mark MacCarthy), 102–06 (Stuart Pratt), 231–32 (Michael Spadea). *See also* Software & Info. Indus. Assoc. Comment #00067, *supra* note 2, at 5–6 and attached report at 7; Tech. Pol'y Inst. Comment #00010, *supra* note 8, at 5–6.

168 Some workshop participants and commenters note other challenges of using utility payments as a non-traditional indicator. *See, e.g.*, Big Data Tr. 51–53 (David Robinson). *See also* Robinson + Yu Comment #00080, *supra* note 53, at 10–11; Nat'l Consumer L. Ctr. Comment #00018, *supra* note 1, at 13–14; Ctr. for Dig. Democracy & U.S. PIRG Educ. Fund Comment #00003, *supra* note 8, at 17.

169 *See, e.g.*, Frank Pasquale, *The Dark Market for Personal Data*, N.Y. Times (Oct. 16, 2014), http://www.nytimes.com/2014/10/17/opinion/the-dark-market-for-personal-data.html?module=Search&mabReward=relbias%3Aw; Danielle Keats Citron, *Big Data Should Be Regulated By 'Technological Due Process,'* N.Y. Times (Aug. 6, 2014), http://www.nytimes.com/roomfordebate/2014/08/06/is-big-data-spreading-inequality/big-data-should-be-regulated-by-technological-due-process; Cathy O'Neil, *The Dark Matter of Big Data*, Mathbabe (June 25, 2014), http://mathbabe.org/2014/06/25/the-dark-matter-of-big-data/; boyd & Crawford, *supra* note 150, at 670–73; Ylan Q. Mui, *Little Known Firms Tracking Data Used in Credit Scores*, Wash. Post (July 16, 2011), http://www.washingtonpost.com/business/economy/little-known-firms-tracking-data-used-in-credit-scores/2011/05/24/gIQAXHcWII_story.html. For the reasons set forth in her separate statement, Commissioner Ohlhausen believes that to assess properly any risks of harm from big data inaccuracies, such risks must be evaluated in the context of the competitive process.

the transaction or be able to correct the information used to flag them as "risky" even if the underlying information was inaccurate.[170]

In using big data to make decisions that affect consumers' ability to complete transactions, companies should consider the potential benefits and harms, especially where their policies could negatively affect certain populations.

4. Does your reliance on big data raise ethical or fairness concerns?

Companies should consider performing their own assessment of the factors that go into an analytics model and balancing the predictive value of the model with fairness considerations.[171] Indeed, overreliance on the predictions of big data analytics could potentially result in a company not thinking critically about the value, fairness, and other implications of their uses of big data.[172] For example, one company determined that employees who live closer to their jobs stay at these jobs longer than those who live farther away.[173] However, another company decided to exclude this factor from its hiring algorithm because of concerns about racial discrimination, particularly since different neighborhoods can have different racial compositions.[174]

Many companies are not only considering ethical concerns with using big data, but are actively using big data to advance the interests of minorities and fight discrimination. For example, there are now recruiting tools available that match companies in search of employees with candidates who hold the necessary qualifications, but also ensure that those candidates are not limited to particular gender, racial, and experiential backgrounds.[175] Individual companies are also changing their hiring techniques to promote

---

170 *See* Data Brokers Report, *supra* note 7, at 53–54.

171 *See, e.g.*, Big Data Tr. 238–40 (Jeanette Fitzgerald). *See generally* The Internet Assoc. Comment #00073, *supra* note 23; Comment #00071 from Pam Dixon, World Privacy Forum, to Fed. Trade Comm'n (Oct. 31, 2014), https://www.ftc.gov/system/files/documents/public_comments/2014/10/00071-92911.pdf; Computer & Commc'ns Indus. Assoc. Comment #00070, *supra* note 141; Consumer Elecs. Assoc. Comment #00068, *supra* note 61; Intel Corp. Comment #00062, *supra* note 61; Comment #00060 from Yael Weinman, Info. Tech. Indus. Council, to Fed. Trade Comm'n (Oct. 27, 2014), https://www.ftc.gov/system/files/documents/public_comments/2014/10/00060-92877.pdf; Info. Accountability Found. Comment #00049, *supra* note 2; Comment #00048 from Bojana Bellamy & Markus Heyder, Ctr. for Info. Pol'y Leadership, to Fed. Trade Comm'n (Oct. 8, 2014), https://www.ftc.gov/system/files/documents/public_comments/2014/10/00048-92775.pdf; Future of Privacy Forum Comment #00027, *supra* note 23.

172 *See, e.g.*, Michael Schrage, *Big Data's Dangerous New Era of Discrimination*, Harv. Bus. Rev. (Jan. 29, 2014), https://hbr.org/2014/01/big-datas-dangerous-new-era-of-discrimination/. *Cf.* Alessandro Acquisti et al., *Face Recognition and Privacy in the Age of Augmented Reality*, 6 J. of Privacy & Confidentiality 1–20 (2014), http://repository.cmu.edu/cgi/viewcontent.cgi?article=1122&context=jpc (showing that big data analytics can now identify strangers online (on a dating site where individuals protect their identities by using pseudonyms) and offline (in a public space), based on photos made publicly available on a social network site, and then infer additional and sensitive information about those consumers with relative ease).

173 *See, e.g.*, Robinson + Yu Comment #00080, *supra* note 53, at 15. *See also* Joseph Walker, *Meet The New Boss: Big Data*, Wall St. J. (Sept. 20, 2012), http://online.wsj.com/news/articles/SB10000872396390443890304578006252019616768.

174 *See supra* note 173.

175 *See, e.g.*, Future of Privacy Forum Comment #00027, *supra* note 23, attached report entitled, Big Data: A Tool for Fighting Discrimination and Empowering Groups, at 1.

diversity.[176] Xerox now uses an online evaluation tool developed by a data analytics firm to assess applicants, in addition to conducting interviews, to determine which applicants are most qualified for available jobs.[177] In developing this new assessment process, Xerox also learned that previous similar employment experience—one of the few criteria that Xerox had explicitly prioritized in the past—turns out to have no bearing on either productivity or retention.[178]

In addition, state and local government entities are using big data to help underrepresented communities obtain better municipal services. For example, states are using big data to identify the needs of lesbian, gay, bisexual, and transgender individuals and to create more tailored approaches to reduce health disparities impacting these individuals.[179] And big data was used to convince a city to redraw its boundaries to extend city services to historically African-American neighborhoods.[180] As these examples show, organizations can use big data in ways that provide opportunity to underrepresented and underserved communities.

Summary of Research Considerations

In light of this research, companies already using or considering engaging in big data analytics should:

- Consider whether your data sets are missing information from particular populations and, if they are, take appropriate steps to address this problem.

- Review your data sets and algorithms to ensure that hidden biases are not having an unintended impact on certain populations.

- Remember that just because big data found a correlation, it does not necessarily mean that the correlation is meaningful. As such, you should balance the risks of using those results, especially where your policies could negatively affect certain populations. It may be worthwhile to have human oversight of data and algorithms when big data tools are used to make important decisions, such as those implicating health, credit, and employment.

- Consider whether fairness and ethical considerations advise against using big data in certain circumstances. Consider further whether you can use big data in ways that advance opportunities for previously underrepresented populations.

---

[176] *See, e.g.*, Tim Smedley, *Forget the CV, Data Decide Careers*, Fin. Times (July 9, 2014), http://www.ft.com/cms/s/2/e3561cd0-dd11-11e3-8546-00144feabdc0.html#axzz373wnekp7.

[177] *See, e.g.*, Peck, *supra* note 143.

[178] *Id.*

[179] *See, e.g.*, Future of Privacy Forum Comment #00027, *supra* note 23, attached report entitled, Big Data: A Tool for Fighting Discrimination and Empowering Groups, at 4; Computer & Commc'ns Indus. Assoc. Comment #00070, *supra* note 141, at 6–7. *See also* Laura Nahmias, *State Agencies Launch LGBT Data-Collection Effort*, Politico N.Y. (July 24, 2014), http://www.capitalnewyork.com/article/albany/2014/07/8549536/state-agencies-launch-lgbt-data-collection-effort.

[180] *See, e.g.*, Future of Privacy Forum Comment #00027, *supra* note 23, attached report entitled, Big Data: A Tool for Fighting Discrimination and Empowering Groups, at 3.

V. Conclusion

Big data will continue to grow in importance, and it is undoubtedly improving the lives of underserved communities in areas such as education, health, local and state services, and employment. Our collective challenge is to make sure that big data analytics continue to provide benefits and opportunities to consumers while adhering to core consumer protection values and principles. For its part, the Commission will continue to monitor areas where big data practices could violate existing laws, including the FTC Act, the FCRA, and ECOA, and will bring enforcement actions where appropriate. In addition, the Commission will continue to examine and raise awareness about big data practices that could have a detrimental impact on low-income and underserved populations and promote the use of big data that has a positive impact on such populations. Given that big data analytics can have big consequences, it is imperative that we work together—government, academics, consumer advocates, and industry—to help ensure that we maximize big data's capacity for good while identifying and minimizing the risks it presents.

Federal Trade Commission

Appendix:
Separate Statement of Commissioner Maureen K. Ohlhausen

Big Data: A Tool for Inclusion or Exclusion?

January 6, 2016

I support today's report on big data as a useful contribution to the ongoing policy discussion about the effect of big data analysis on low-income, disadvantaged, and vulnerable consumers. One part of the report summarizes the concerns of several privacy advocates and academics over the potential inaccuracies of big data analytics. I write separately to emphasize the importance of evaluating these opinions in the context of market and competitive forces that affect all companies using big data analytics.

The report details the use of big data as it affects low-income, disadvantaged, or vulnerable consumers. Importantly, the report describes some of the many ways companies are already using big data to benefit such consumers—and others. The report also recognizes big data's massive potential benefits. In addition, the report sketches the legal landscape implicated by big data and offers questions that companies may find useful as they apply big data techniques to solve their business challenges.

The report also describes certain concerns about big data tools raised by some consumer advocates and researchers. Specifically, some fear that big data analysis will produce inaccurate or incomplete results, and that actions based on such flawed analysis will harm low-income, disadvantaged, or vulnerable consumers.[1] For example, some worry that companies may use inaccurate big data analysis to deny opportunities to otherwise eligible low-income or disadvantaged consumers, or to fail to advertise high-quality lending products to eligible low-income customers.[2]

Concerns about the effects of inaccurate data are certainly legitimate, but policymakers must evaluate such concerns in the larger context of the market and economic forces companies face. Businesses have strong incentives to seek accurate information about consumers, whatever the tool. Indeed, businesses use big data specifically to increase accuracy. Our competition expertise tells us that if one company draws incorrect conclusions and misses opportunities, competitors with better analysis will strive to fill the gap.[3]

---

1   FED. TRADE COMM'N, BIG DATA: A TOOL FOR INCLUSION OR EXCLUSION? UNDERSTANDING THE ISSUES 8–11, 25–27 (2016). The report also references other concerns that big data analysis will be *too* accurate: companies will understand their consumers too well and misuse that data to the consumer's detriment. Market forces also constrain many such potential harms, but other such harms could actually undermine market forces. For example, the report describes concerns that unscrupulous businesses will use big data techniques to develop "sucker lists" of consumers particularly vulnerable to scams and misleading offers. The report does a good job laying out the existing legal framework that applies to such harmful uses.

2   *Id.* at 9–11.

3   A real world example of the competitive advantages of novel but accurate application of data analytics was famously chronicled in the book (and movie) *Moneyball*. *See* MICHAEL LEWIS, MONEYBALL: THE ART OF WINNING AN UNFAIR GAME (2004). Oakland's strategy succeeded precisely because it "liberated" baseball players from "unthinking prejudice rooted in baseball's traditions . . . allowing them to demonstrate their true worth." *Id.* at iiv. Each baseball franchise continually faces

Therefore, to the extent that companies today misunderstand members of low-income, disadvantaged, or vulnerable populations, big data analytics combined with a competitive market may well *resolve* these misunderstandings rather than *perpetuate* them.[4] In particular, a company's failure to communicate premium offers to eligible consumers presents a prime business opportunity for a competitor with a better algorithm.[5]

To understand the benefits and risks of tools like big data analytics, we must also consider the powerful forces of economics and free-market competition. If we give undue credence to hypothetical harms, we risk distracting ourselves from genuine harms and discouraging the development of the very tools that promise new benefits to low income, disadvantaged, and vulnerable individuals.

Today's report enriches the conversation about big data. My hope is that future participants in this conversation will test hypothetical harms with economic reasoning and empirical evidence.[6]

---

marketplace pressures to improve player quality predictions. Similarly, companies using big data analytics face competitive forces that punish inaccuracy and reward accuracy.

4   Indeed, there is strong theoretical and empirical economic evidence that low income and other disadvantaged households stand to gain more than the wealthy from many applications of big data analytics. *See* JAMES C. COOPER, SEPARATION, POOLING, AND PREDICTIVE PRIVACY HARMS FROM BIG DATA: CONFUSING BENEFITS FOR COSTS 38–49 (2015), http://ssrn.com/abstract=2655794 (describing theoretical and empirical studies on the effects of big data in credit markets, price discrimination, and labor markets for low income individuals). One simple example: lenders do not need big data analytics to identify creditworthy high-income persons, as nearly all have credit files and most are lower-risk. However, lower-income groups contain both high- and low-risk borrowers. Big data analysis can help bring credit to the lower-risk low income borrowers with thin or no credit files. *See id.* at 38–39.

5   Transcript of Big Data: A Tool for Inclusion or Exclusion?, in Washington, D.C. (Sept. 15, 2014), at 231–32 (Daniel Castro and Michael Spaeda in conversation), https://www.ftc.gov/system/files/documents/public_events/313371/bigdata-transcript-9_15_14.pdf (highlighting the business opportunities in improved accuracy of credit scoring for low-income individuals). Indeed, our workshop on lead generation showed that lenders and other businesses are highly motivated to reach potential customers and spend a lot of money and effort to do so. *See generally Follow the Lead: An FTC Workshop on Lead Generation*, FED. TRADE COMM'N (Oct. 30, 2015), https://www.ftc.gov/news-events/events-calendar/2015/10/follow-lead-ftc-workshop-lead-generation.

6   For example, Cooper describes a useful framework to help identify under which conditions the presumption should be for or against big data uses. *See* COOPER, *supra* note 4, at 33–38.